Physical Characteristics of the
Australian Cattle Dog
(from the American Kennel Club breed standard)

Body: The length of the body from the point of the breast bone, in a straight line to the buttocks, is greater than the height at the withers, as 10 is to 9. The topline is level, back strong with ribs well sprung and carried well back.

Loins: Broad, strong and muscular.

Tail: The set on of tail is moderately low, following the contours of the sloping croup and of length to reach approximately to the hock.

Hindquarters: Broad, strong and muscular. The croup is rather long and sloping, thighs long, broad and well developed, the stifles well turned and the hocks strong and well let down.

Coat: Smooth, a double coat with a short dense undercoat. The outer coat is close, each hair straight, hard, and lying flat, so that it is rain-resisting. As an average, the hairs on the body should be from 2.5 to 4 cms (approx. 1–1.5 ins) in length.

Feet: Should be round and the toes short, strong, well arched and held close together. The pads are hard and deep, and the nails must be short and strong.

Australian Cattle Dog

◇

By Charlotte Schwartz

Contents

KENNEL CLUB BOOKS® **AUSTRALIAN CATTLE DOG**
ISBN: 1-59378-368-X

Copyright © 2004, 2007 • Kennel Club Books, LLC
308 Main Street, Allenhurst, NJ 07711 USA
Cover Design Patented: US 6,435,559 B2 • Printed in South Korea

Photographs by Michael Trafford, with additional photos by:
Norvia Behling, Bernd Brinkmann, T.J. Calhoun, Carolina Biological Supply, Doskocil,
W. P. Fleming/Viesti Associates, Isabelle Français, James Hayden-Yoav, James R. Hayden, RBP,
Carol Ann Johnson, Bill Jonas, Dwight R. Kuhn, Dr. Dennis Kunkel, Mikki Pet Products,
Phototake, Jean Claude Revy, Alice Roche, Dr. Andrew Spielman and Alice van Kempen.

Illustrations by Patricia Peters.

The publisher would like to thank all of the owners of the dogs featured in this book, including
Vicki L. Anderson, Debbie Clark, Diana Durrance, Kimberley Jebson/Austman Kennels,
Patty Kasper, Carol Anne Kriesel, Robert and Margaret Loring, Cindy Muir, Kelly Rea,
Narelle Robertson/Kombinalong Kennels, Sherry Toft and Marja Vornanen.

10 9 8 7 6 5 4 3

The well-bred Kombinalong Born to be Super is a great example of what an Australian Cattle Dog should be. At only five months old, "Kylie" is working cattle in the breed's homeland.

HISTORY OF THE
AUSTRALIAN CATTLE DOG

The land rolls on for miles ahead of you. The grass is dry, brown, summer-hot and barely moving in a breeze that just can't get started. Cattle begin to stir. A small dark figure appears out of nowhere and begins to circle the herd. The dog is going to work. From somewhere off in the distance, a series of sharp whistle notes tells the dog to start the herd moving toward the river.

Some cattle balk at the orders. Quickly, the dog convinces them to move out. As they do, dust rises up from the ground and, momentarily, the dog is lost in the cloud. Can you picture the dust rising? The cattle synchronizing their movement? The occasional cow that refuses to stay with the herd?

Watch the dog and you'll see what he does best. Seeing a cow drifting away, the dog races up behind the animal. With lightning speed, he bites the hock of the cow's rear leg. Instantly, dust flies again. The errant cow lashes out at the dog with flying hooves. But the dog is safe.

Years of careful breeding have insured that the dog will bite, then duck low beneath those driving hooves. When the cow's hooves thrash back and upward, the dog drops below the cow's line of fire. Inbred instinct keeps the dog safe to drive the herd another day. Training tells him how to enforce the herdsman's orders.

You have been privy to an amazing display of a dog working together with man to accomplish what the man alone could never do. The dog is an Australian Cattle Dog.

Just as the name implies, the Australian Cattle Dog is a tough, fearless, loyal, all-business kind of dog. In action and at a distance, he looks like a miniature tank with fur. He goes where others dare not go, he's unstoppable and he's afraid of nothing. These traits also make him a devoted companion to his owner and a dedicated protector of the home.

He's been bred for herding cattle in Australia since the early 1800s, when settlers realized they needed a dog to help them move and control the cattle in the open country, where there were no fences. Initially, it took years of experimenting with various breeds of dog to produce what we know today as the Australian Cattle Dog or Blue Heeler.

Back in those early days, ranchers used bob-tailed dogs called "Smithfields" to round up and herd the wild cattle that roamed the bush country. However, the Smithfields possessed some traits that the ranchers didn't like. They barked almost constantly, bit too hard when working the herds and did not cope well with the extreme heat of the outback.

The year 1830 saw the beginning of a series of experimental matings of various breeds of dog to get the desired traits needed in the cattle dog. First, a man named Timmins from a town north of Sydney crossed his dogs with a Dingo, the native wild dog of Australia. The pups were quiet, quick and a great improvement over the Smithfields. However, they possessed one serious fault—when beyond the supervision of a drover, some of their inherited Dingo traits caused them to bite and chew the cows so severely that the animals could not be marketed. The Stumpy Tail Cattle Dog derived from Timmins' stock.

More experimental breedings followed. Mixes of Collies, Bull Terriers, Welsh Herders, Kangaroo Dogs and Russian Poodles were tried. None of these crosses

DOG-UMENTATION

Did you know that documenting the existence of dog breeds can be done in various ways? For example, literature, ancient artwork, spoken stories, songs, riddles and even children's games often help to document certain breeds and the dates when they became popular.

The Dingo is one of the four breeds that made up the original Australian Cattle Dog.

worked satisfactorily for herding cattle. Biting and chewing the cattle was unacceptable. Excessive barking served to rattle the cattle; thus, the cows became unmanageable. Some of the crosses suffered so greatly from the extreme heat of the rugged terrain that they were drained of energy and unable to work the long hours required.

Then, in 1840, a rancher by the name of Thomas Hall, of New South Wales, began experimenting with a combination of Welsh Heelers and Dingos. The resulting puppies proved to be exactly what the cattle drovers needed. The pups, known as Hall's Heelers, worked quietly and quickly, and they only nipped at the heels of straggling cows rather than ravaging them. In addition, they exhibited a desirable Dingo trait: They crept up silently on the cattle, nipped their fetlocks to get them moving and immediately flattened themselves on the ground to prevent being kicked by flying hooves.

Drovers and graziers alike approved of Hall's Heelers. The dogs possessed long-distance stamina and the ability to cope

GENUS *CANIS*

Dogs and wolves are members of the genus *Canis*. Wolves are known scientifically as *Canis lupus* while dogs are known as *Canis domesticus*. Dogs and wolves are known to interbreed. The term "canine" derives from the Latin-derived word *Canis*. The term "dog" has no scientific basis but has been used for thousands of years. The origin of the word "dog" has never been authoritatively ascertained.

with the extreme heat, and the rugged terrain never stopped them from moving and controlling the cattle. The dogs, it seemed, could work anywhere, anytime, under any conditions. The Welsh Heelers of Scotland and the Dingos of Australia apparently were the winning combination.

In appearance, the dogs looked like shorter, heavier-set versions of Dingos. In color, they were either a rich red or blue merle, a mottled blend of black and white. They had broad skulls, brown eyes and pricked ears that emerged from the corners of their wedge-shaped heads. Overall, they portrayed the image of powerful working dogs, possessing great stamina and agility.

The Kelpie is another Australian native, added to the AuCaDo mix for working ability.

About the same time, a Queensland rancher named George Elliot produced some outstanding herding dogs, also mixes of Collies and Dingos. Their pups, too, were in great demand and soon appeared in Sydney markets, working the cattle in confined spaces as well as on the vast ranges of the outback.

The cattle sale yards were the proving grounds for Hall's Heelers when Fred Davis, a butcher, used them to move the cattle from one small yard to another as the animals came up for sale. Seeing the outstanding ability of his dogs, Davis began breeding them. Soon two brothers, Jack and Harry Bagust, purchased some of the Davis pups and began breeding them with an eye to perfecting their working ability.

First, they crossed one of their blue merle bitches with a Dalmatian, which changed the blue merle to blue speckled, the color and pattern that is known today. The purpose of introducing Dalmatian genes was to enhance the dogs' ability to work with horses and strengthen their devotion to their masters.

Finally, to reinforce a strong working driver, the Bagusts introduced Australian Kelpie blood into their dogs. Bred to herd and control sheep, Kelpies are superior herders, extremely intelligent and easily controlled. In appearance, the breed resembles a heav-

Aust. Gr. Ch. Kombinalong Super Octane, the youngest Grand Champion in the breed, with owner/breeder Narelle Robertson.

ier version of the Dingo. Along with the blue or red speckling, modern Cattle Dogs carry red or blue patches around their eyes, which they inherited from the Kelpie.

Once the newest Blue Heelers were genetically set in looks, temperament and working ability, they attracted the interest of a man named Robert Kaleski, a journalist and dog fancier. In 1893, Kaleski began breeding the Blue Heelers and, by 1897, he introduced them at dog shows for the first time. Since no more experimental breeding was done after the infusion of the Kelpie, Kaleski wrote the standard for the breed in 1902 and submitted it to the Cattle and Sheep Dog Club of Australia and the Kennel Club of New South Wales for approval. The standard was approved in 1903.

Eventually, the breed assumed the official name of Australian

Cattle Dog. In addition to being known as Blue Heelers or Queensland Heelers, they're often referred to as Blueys.

In the United States, the breed was accepted for registration by the American Kennel Club in 1980, and they are officially recognized as Australian Cattle Dogs. The term "AuCaDo" is another name used for the Australian Cattle Dog in America. Whatever they're called or wherever they live, this hardy breed has changed little from the dog it was in the early 1900s. That fact has served the breed well in keeping it free of genetic problems often seen in other breeds subjected to breed tampering.

NIPPING COUSINS

The AuCaDo's lesser known cousin is known as the Stumpy Tail Cattle Dog, originally referred to as the Timmins Biter. The breed was created by a cattleman by the name of Timmins, who crossed the native bobtailed Smithfield, Dingo and a blue-merle Smooth Collie. Once thought to be a variant of the AuCaDo, the Stumpy Tail is not an Aussie spinoff without a tail. The breed does not derive from the Kelpie, as does the AuCaDo, and there are some important conformational differences. The Stumpy Tail cannot have tan markings, has a more wedge-shaped, less broad head, has a square body, high-set smaller ears and an undocked, natural "stumpy" tail.

An example of the consistent type and quality of the breed world-wide is this beautiful Australian Cattle Dog from the UK.

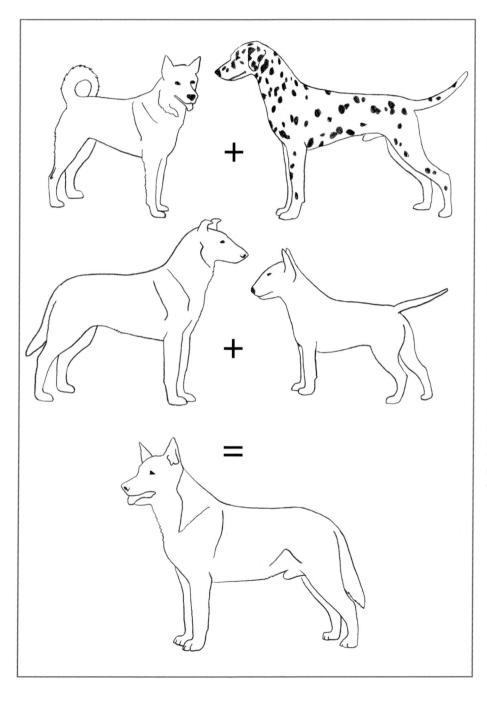

The Australian Cattle Dog (bottom) incorporated existing Australian working dogs with the following: Dingo (upper left), a native wild dog, for endurance and athletic ability; Dalmatian (upper right), for affinity for horses and humans and for sound running gear; Smooth Collie (middle left), for herding ability and affinity for and loyalty to humans; Bull Terrier (middle right) for just a touch of toughness and aggression to deal with free-range, undomesticated cattle.

CHARACTERISTICS OF THE
AUSTRALIAN CATTLE DOG

IS THE AUSTRALIAN CATTLE DOG RIGHT FOR YOU?

In every breed of dog, there are certain characteristics that set that breed apart, separating it from all other breeds of dog. These characteristics form the defining signature that stamps the dog as a specific breed, even though the individual dog is also a member of the canine species. Breed-specific characteristics are a breed's mark of distinction. These comprise how the dog looks, the way he acts and the subtle little (and sometimes big!) mannerisms that he exhibits in daily life.

Frequently, such habits as high-pitched, excited barking are genetically engineered into the dog for a reason. Shetland Sheepdogs, for example, bark in this manner when they're herding. Dachshunds often bark when they go to ground in their hunt for vermin. Once underground and out of the owner's sight, the yipping of the Dachshund helps the owner keep track of his dog's whereabouts.

In the case of the Australian Cattle Dog, there are a number of important physical and behavioral characteristics that set the dog apart from all others. First, the AuCaDo is extremely intelligent, capable of making decisions regarding himself, his owner and family, his job and his home territory. This ability is a result of a combination of his instincts, experiences, intellect and innate desire to function effectively within his own pack.

Probably the best way to get to learn about a particular breed of dog is to talk with those who own members of the breed. In the case of the Australian Cattle Dog, characteristic traits are never kept secret. Owners are eager to share what they know about their dogs and even more anxious to have you understand that the AuCaDo is not the right breed for everyone.

Owners will tell you that the Australian Cattle Dog is courageous, alert, curious and capable of long hours of hard work in rugged conditions. He's athletic, quiet, versatile and aloof. His protective instincts are strong; his loyalty to his master and family and his home and property are without question.

The AuCaDo is strong-willed, selective in making friends, suspicious of strangers and aggressive when he, his family or his home is threatened. On the other hand, he loves children, is playful and eager to please and requires a firm but gentle type of discipline in management and training. Most of all, he is not a couch potato and will never be content to live a sedentary life with just a short walk around the block every day.

This high-energy dog wants to work, needs to work and works superbly at whatever task he is taught to perform. He has tireless energy that must be channeled into productive behavior every day of his life. A hike in the park on Sundays will not satisfy this working dog. He must live a full, active life with a master he loves and respects.

Unlike some breeds of dog whose characteristics are spelled out in one paragraph of the breed standard, the AuCaDo's characteristics are listed in detail and at great length. For example, included in the characteristics of the breed, emphasis is placed on the fact that AuCaDo puppies should be placed in their new homes before they reach adolescence. This way, they will develop strong bonds with their masters, with whom they will permanently live (and possibly work). Adult AuCaDos do not do well in cases in which they must change homes and masters once they reach maturity. Their bond is for life, and they do not adjust easily to new owners once they become adult dogs.

Furthermore, it is so important that AuCaDo puppies

WHAT'S THAT "SOUND"?
Did you know that the word "soundness" used in describing a breed of dog refers not only to the physical makeup of that breed but also to a sound temperament, thus making the dog's personality characteristics predictable.

begin their lives in appropriate homes that the details of the dogs' needs are given high importance in the breed standard. If placed inappropriately in homes where they will not be given jobs to do, the dogs will likely end up being shifted from home to home because they develop undesirable behavior problems. Sometimes these problems become so severe that the dogs are turned over to animal shelters and cannot be rehomed.

Who, then, makes an ideal AuCaDo owner? Obviously, it's a

Living on a farm is not a prerequisite to AuCaDo ownership, but the ideal owner will provide outlets for her dog's energy. Training for and participating in various areas of the dog sport are great ways to keep the breed mentally and physically challenged.

person who has the time and need for a working dog. Since the dog is an active one, a large property such as a farm or ranch makes for a perfect home where the dog can perform daily tasks to help his master around the property. Again, it must be emphasized that Australian Cattle Dogs do not make good house pets that will "hang out" around the home and do nothing most of the time. They need to have a meaningful purpose in life to be well-adjusted companions. If his requirements are met, the AuCaDo will make a lifelong friend, devoted to his master and family.

Physically, the Australian Cattle Dog must be first and foremost a sound dog. He is a compact, muscular dog with great strength. Correct physical structure allows the dog to be supple, quick, athletic and capable of tireless effort for prolonged durations. In short, the AuCaDo is an athlete in the truest sense of the word. Without these attributes, he will not be able to perform his job, thus making him useless as a working companion. And let it be understood that a good, well-trained Australian Cattle Dog can often do the work of several ranch hands without even breaking a sweat.

I recall the time I spent on a large property in Tasmania, Australia. One day, I was watching an AuCaDo working with some cattle, when a cantankerous bull kicked him in the side and sent the dog flying many feet away. When he hit the ground, the dog rolled over, stood up, shook his head and came back with a vengeance to bite the hock of the bull. As his teeth made contact with the bovine's hind leg, the no-longer-stubborn bull turned and jogged away just as the dog had originally indicated for him to do. Suddenly that 1500-pound bull became a docile critter at the mercy of a determined dog!

Once you witness an Australian Cattle Dog at work, you gain a surprising respect for the breed. It's amazing to witness such an intelligent animal, doing what he's bred to do and doing it

The Australian Cattle Dog loves children and the feeling is mutual; but, at the same time, the breed is strong-willed and may attempt to herd toddlers.

HEART HEALTHY

The *Australian Medical Journal* in 1992 found that having pets is heart-healthy. Pet owners had lower blood pressure and lower levels of triglycerides than those who didn't have pets. It has also been found that senior citizens who own pets are more active and less likely to experience depression than those without pets.

so well. It's then that you realize that this dog would be absolutely miserable in any other type of lifestyle. He needs to do what he loves most to do—*work*.

Owner Mary Ann Mullen, who lives in Virginia, loves to tell people about her Australian Cattle Dog, Cassie. The dog's registered American Kennel Club name is R-Bar's Roshara Mama Cass, UDX, NA, HIC. She has earned the coveted Utility Dog Excellent title in obedience competition, plus a Novice Agility title, and she's Herding Instinct Certified. At six years of age, Cassie keeps busy despite the fact that Ms. Mullen does not live on a large property. Cassie does not herd livestock, but her many other activities replace the usual farm work and provide that necessary feeling of fulfillment.

"Cattle Dogs have extremely strong chase instincts and movement of any kind serves as a trigger," says Ms. Mullen. "As much as they love children and will guard them as their own, I don't recommend getting an Australian Cattle Dog for a family with little children. The dogs frequently nip at the flying feet of the children in an attempt to herd the kids and keep them all together. Older children do well with the dogs and strong bonds of affection, minus the nipping, develop easily."

Ms. Mullen contributes another important recommendation: "Australian Cattle Dogs are not for the first-time dog owner. They must be trained in basic manners and control and an experienced dog owner is better equipped to accomplish this. The dogs can be stubborn and need firm guidance from an owner who realizes they are not little people in fur coats."

Cattle Dogs are not for everyone. They're stoic and need to be understood and respected by owners who have some knowledge of basic dog behavior. Once you understand them, you'll admire their serious nature and devotion to home and family. In the correct environment, Australian Cattle Dogs make superb companions for life.

PHYSICAL PROBLEMS OF CONCERN

As with most breeds of dogs, there are some hereditary and congenital problems that have been seen

Even the most stoic Australian Cattle Dog appreciates a cuddle with the owner he loves.

in AuCaDos. For example, deafness is occasionally identified in the breed. This condition is probably caused by the Dalmatian genes and is often identified when the dogs are puppies.

Some dogs are deaf in both ears, some in only one. Puppy ear canals do not open until the puppies are around two weeks of age, so evaluating them should not be done until the puppies are five to eight weeks of age. BAER (brainstem auditory evoked response) testing is an electrodiagnostic test that can be performed on puppies younger than this age, but limited availability of testing sites make this prohibitive in many cases.

In the case of total deafness, there is a poor probability that the dog will enjoy a full and rewarding life. Most breeders will euthanize puppies that are totally deaf. Partial deafness, however, does not tend to be as devastating to the dog once he reaches maturity since the dog learns to compensate for his disability.

Hip dysplasia (HD) is another area of concern. In this condition, the hip joint is misaligned so that the ball of the thigh bone does not sit correctly into the socket of the hip. Each time the joint is moved, bone rubs on bone, creating a painful and debilitating condition. In some severe cases, surgery can alleviate the dog's discomfort, but it cannot create a new joint.

Frequently seen in many dog breeds, HD must be identified via radiographic diagnosis by a veterinary expert. Sending the resulting film to an evaluating organization will result in getting the dog's hips graded and his grades registered with that organization. The OFA, Orthopedic Foundation for Animals, certifies various levels of HD and allots a grade of involvement to each case. There are other certifying organizations for HD in other countries. Since HD is hereditary, dogs with HD should not be bred, as the puppies will probably carry the problem as well. In short, only dogs who obtain hip scores that certify them as free of HD should be bred.

Luxating patella is another name for dislocated knee joints. As with HD, the problem can be severe and is hereditary. Passing on this painful condition to the dog's puppies is cruel. Therefore, dogs affected with patellar luxation problems should never be bred.

Finally, we need to mention the degenerative eye disease known as progressive retinal atrophy (PRA). Sometimes referred to as night blindness, PRA causes the retinal cells to deteriorate so that the back of the eye no longer is capable of sending electrical signals to the brain. The nerves atrophy and the dog becomes blind.

The onset of this condition is often observed when the dog stumbles into things at night and seems unable to get his bearings. During bright daylight, however, the dog seems to be fine. Unfortunately, there is no cure for PRA and the condition usually reaches its peak when the dog is between the age of four and eight years.

A veterinary ophthalmologist is the only person qualified to test for PRA and can detect it in very young puppies. Both parents must carry the gene for PRA, but when only one parent carries the gene, it is considered autosomal. In that case, some of the puppies will show signs of PRA, some will merely carry the gene and a few will be clear of PRA. Therefore, buying a puppy from certified clear parents is the only way to assure yourself of having a dog with no potential for PRA.

Despite these physical problems seen in Australian Cattle Dogs, they are a far cry from some breeds in which the reported health problems are counted in the dozens. The way to avoid these conditions to the best of your ability is to purchase your AuCaDo puppy from a reputable breeder who tests the parents and puppies for known health and hereditary problems.

DO YOU KNOW ABOUT HIP DYSPLASIA?

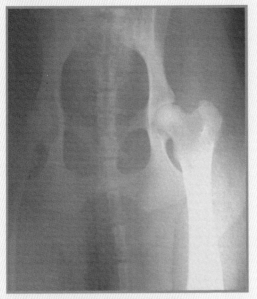

X-ray of a dog with "Good" hips.

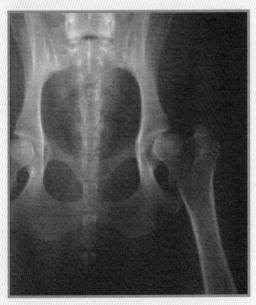

X-ray of a dog with "Moderate" dysplastic hips.

Hip dysplasia is a fairly common condition found in pure-bred dogs. When a dog has hip dysplasia, his hind leg has an incorrectly formed hip joint. By constant use of the hip joint, it becomes more and more loose, wears abnormally and may become arthritic.

Hip dysplasia can only be confirmed with an x-ray, but certain symptoms may indicate a problem. Your dog may have a hip dysplasia problem if he walks in a peculiar manner, hops instead of smoothly runs, uses his hind legs in unison (to keep the pressure off the weak joint), has trouble getting up from a prone position or always sits with both legs together on one side of his body.

As the dog matures, he may adapt well to life with a bad hip, but in a few years the arthritis develops and many dogs with hip dysplasia become crippled.

Hip dysplasia is considered an inherited disease and only can be diagnosed definitively by x-ray when the dog is two years old, although symptoms often appear earlier. Some experts claim that a special diet might help your puppy outgrow the bad hip, but the usual treatments are surgical. The removal of the pectineus muscle, the removal of the round part of the femur, reconstructing the pelvis and replacing the hip with an artificial one are all surgical interventions that are expensive, but they are usually very successful. Follow the advice of your veterinarian.

AUSTRALIAN CATTLE DOG

The standard of perfection for a specific breed of dog gives detailed information about how the breed should look. The physical conformation of a breed is described by the parent club of that breed and usually includes more than just a cursory explanation of the dog's general appearance.

Behavioral characteristics are often included in the description. Statements that help to define the breed are important to anyone seeking a representative example of that particular breed. Words like "an impression of strength and agility" help clarify the typical example of a breed. Characteristics such as "suspicious of strangers" and "dedicated to home and family" enhance one's understanding of just what makes up the total dog of any given breed. The standard of perfection is superbly spelled out for the Australian Cattle Dog.

Once the parent club composes the standard, kennel clubs around the world use that as a guideline by which to judge dogs of that breed. Thus, physical conformation plus personality and behavioral traits all add up to create the blueprint for the breed's future.

In the case of the Australian Cattle Dog, breeders have been so specific regarding the breed standard that whole pages of descriptions have been written about the breed. It is obvious that the originators of the Australian Cattle Dog wanted to be very clear in their definition in order to avoid future mistakes in identifying the AuCaDo. Thus, with a clearly spelled out description, future breeders would have specific guidelines to follow in producing succeeding generations

WHERE DOES A STANDARD COME FROM?

Did you know that AKC breed standards are written by each breed's parent club? Those standards are then used by dog-show judges to determine the dog or dogs that come closest to that criteria in their task of choosing the winners on any particular day. Standard are also used by breeders in creating breeding programs to produce the highest quality puppies that will grow up to become correct representatives of their breed.

that were exact replicas of the original dog.

For example, in its description of the ears, specific mention is made of the inside of the ear: "...ears should be fairly well furnished with hair." The reason? In the dirt and dust of the outback, hair on the inside of the dog's ears helps to keep foreign matter from getting into the ear canal.

In reference to the feet, the standard writers included mention of the nails: "Nails must be short and strong." It is essential that the dog have short, strong nails to give him traction when herding cattle in the rough terrain of a farm or ranch property. Long delicate toenails would break and cause great suffering to the ill-equipped dog.

This attention to detail has served the breed well ever since the original standard was written by Robert Kaleski in 1902. The breed standard was first approved by the Australian Cattle Dog Club of America on June 12, 1979. The current standard, which is presented here, was revised and approved on January 11, 1999. Committed to the breed's ability as well as conformation, the parent club also has a Working-dog standard that describes the purpose, intelligence, trainability, posture, approach, eye, grip and bark of the AuCaDo. This can be viewed on the website (www.acdca.org).

Judges use a "hands-on" approach in examining each dog for correct structure from tail to teeth.

THE AMERICAN KENNEL CLUB BREED STANDARD FOR THE AUSTRALIAN CATTLE DOG

General Appearance: The general appearance is that of a strong, compact, symmetrically built working dog, with the ability and willingness to carry out his allotted task however arduous. Its combination of substance, power, balance and hard muscular condition must convey the impression of great agility, strength and endurance. Any tendency to grossness or weediness is a serious fault.

Characteristics: As the name implies, the dog's prime function, and one in which he has no peer, is the control and movement of cattle in both wide open and confined areas. Always alert,

An Australian Cattle Dog in profile, showing correct type, balance, structure and substance.

extremely intelligent, watchful, courageous and trustworthy, with an implicit devotion to duty making it an ideal dog.

Temperament: The Cattle Dog's loyalty and protective instincts make it a self-appointed guardian to the Stockman, his herd and his property. Whilst naturally suspicious of strangers, must be amenable to handling, particularly in the Show ring. Any feature of temperament or structure foreign to a working dog must be regarded as a serious fault.

Head: The head is strong and must be in balance with other proportions of the dog and in keeping with its general conformation. The broad skull is slightly curved between the ears, flattening to a slight but definite stop. The cheeks muscular, neither coarse nor prominent with the underjaw strong, deep and well developed. The foreface is broad and well filled in under the eyes, tapering gradually to form a medium length, deep, powerful muzzle with the skull and muzzle on parallel planes.

The lips are tight and clean. Nose black.

Eyes—The eyes should be of oval shape and medium size, neither prominent nor sunken and must express alertness and intelligence. A warning or suspicious glint is characteristic when approached by strangers. Eye color, dark brown. *Ears*—The ears should be of moderate size, preferably small rather than large, broad at the base, muscular, pricked and moderately pointed, neither spoon nor bat eared. The ears are set wide apart on the skull, inclining outwards, sensitive in their use and pricked when alert, the leather should be thick in texture and the inside of the ear fairly well furnished with hair. *Mouth*—The teeth, sound, strong and evenly spaced, gripping with a scissor-bite, the lower incisors close behind and just touching the upper. As the dog is required to move difficult cattle by heeling or biting, teeth which are sound and strong are very important.

Neck: The neck is extremely strong, muscular, and of medium length broadening to blend into the body and free from throatiness.

Head study, showing correct structure, balance and type.

Forequarters: The shoulders are strong, sloping, muscular and well angulated to the upper arm and should not be too closely set at the point of the withers. The forelegs have strong, round bone, extending to the feet and should be straight and parallel when viewed from the front, but the pasterns should show flexibility with a slight angle to the forearm when viewed from the side. Although the shoulders are muscular and the bone is strong, loaded shoulders and heavy fronts will hamper correct movement and limit working ability.

Body: The length of the body from the point of the breast bone, in a straight line to the buttocks, is greater than the height at the withers, as 10 is to 9. The topline is level, back strong with ribs well sprung and carried well back, not barrel ribbed. The chest is deep, muscular and moderately broad with the loins broad, strong and muscular and the flanks deep. The dog is strongly coupled.

Hindquarters: The hindquarters are broad, strong and muscular. The croup is rather long and sloping, thighs long, broad and

Aust. Ch. Kombinalong Daretobsuper, bred by Kombinalong Kennels.

well developed, the stifles well turned and the hocks strong and well let down. When viewed from behind, the hind legs, from the hocks to the feet, are straight and placed parallel, neither close nor too wide apart.

Feet: The feet should be round and the toes short, strong, well arched and held close together. The pads are hard and deep, and the nails must be short and strong.

Tail: The set on of tail is moderately low, following the contours of the sloping croup and of length to reach approximately to the hock. At rest it should hang in a very slight curve. During movement or excitement the tail may be raised, but under no circumstances should any part of the tail be carried past a vertical line drawn through the root. The tail should carry a good brush.

FAULTS IN PROFILE

Generally lacking substance, long back, upright shoulders, ewe neck, weak pasterns, flat feet.

Lacking athletic flexibility, coarse, thick and loaded shoulders, high in the rear, long back.

A proper Cattle Dog scissors bite.

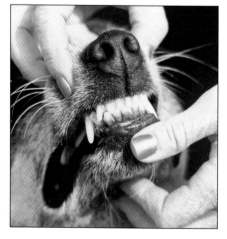

Gait/Movement: The action is true, free, supple and tireless and the movement of the shoulders and forelegs is in unison with the powerful thrust of the hindquarters. The capability of quick and sudden movement is essential. Soundness is of paramount importance and stiltiness, loaded or slack shoulders, straight shoulder placement, weakness at elbows, pasterns or feet, straight stifles, cow or bow hocks, must be regarded as serious faults. When trotting the feet tend to come closer together at ground level as speed increases, but when the dog comes to rest he should stand four square.

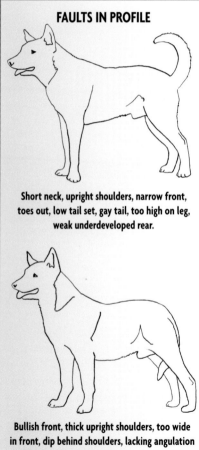

FAULTS IN PROFILE

Short neck, upright shoulders, narrow front, toes out, low tail set, gay tail, too high on leg, weak underdeveloped rear.

Bullish front, thick upright shoulders, too wide in front, dip behind shoulders, lacking angulation behind, tail carriage indicating questionable temperament.

The breed's athleticism and stamina should be evident in the proper gait, which is among the points evaluated at conformation shows.

Coat: The coat is smooth, a double coat with a short dense undercoat. The outer coat is close, each hair straight, hard, and lying flat, so that it is rain-resisting. Under the body, to behind the legs, the coat is longer and forms near the thigh a mild form of breeching. On the head (including the inside of the ears), to the front of the legs and feet, the hair is short. Along the neck it is longer and thicker. A coat either too long or too short is a fault. As an average, the hairs on the body should be from 2.5 to 4 cms (approx. 1–1.5 ins) in length.

Color (Blue): The color should be blue, blue-mottled or blue speckled with or without other markings. The permissible markings are black, blue or tan markings on the head, evenly distributed for preference. The forelegs tan midway up the legs and extending up the front to

A close-up of the Cattle Dog's smooth double coat. The short, dense outer coat is made up of straight, hard, flat-lying hairs.

breast and throat, with tan on jaws; the hindquarters tan on inside of hindlegs, and inside of thighs, showing down the front of the stifles and broadening out to the outside of the hindlegs from hock to toes. Tan undercoat is permissible on the body providing it does not show through the blue outer coat. Black markings on the body are not desirable.

Color (Red Speckle): The color should be of good even red speckle all over, including the undercoat (neither white nor cream), with or without darker red markings on the head. Even head markings are desirable. Red markings on the body are permissible but not desirable.

Size: Height: Dogs 46–51 cms (approx. 18–20 ins) at withers. Bitches 43–48 cms (approx. 17–19 ins) at withers.

Faults: Any departure from the foregoing points should be considered a fault and the seriousness with which the fault should be regarded should be in exact proportion to its degree.

Approved: January 11, 1999
Effective: February 24, 1999

Ch. Gravans Snow Spryte, owned by Carol Anne Kriesel and bred by Sissi Vance, is a daughter of Aust., Am., Mex., Guat., Belize, Int. Ch. Kombinalong Super Impact.

AUSTRALIAN CATTLE DOG

SELECTING AND PREPARING FOR YOUR PUPPY

Here comes an important event in your life! You're about to find the Australian Cattle Dog that's perfect for you and your lifestyle. Keep in mind that your selection should be based on the homework you've done prior to this time. In other words, you've researched the breed by reading as much as you can on the subject, talking to AuCaDo breeders and getting their advice regarding whether or not the AuCaDo is the right breed of dog for you and, finally, talking to

YOUR SCHEDULE . . .
If you lead an erratic, unpredictable life, with daily or weekly changes in your work requirements, consider the problems of owning a puppy. The new puppy has to be fed regularly, socialized (loved, petted, handled, introduced to other people) and, most importantly, allowed to go outdoors for house-training. As the dog gets older, he can be more tolerant of deviations in his feeding and relief schedule.

other Australian Cattle Dog owners and heeding their comments on the breed. The parent club for the breed, the Australian Cattle Dog Club of America (www.acdca.org) is a good source of information and can point you to regional clubs and member breeders in your part of the country. Additionally, it would be wise to talk to your local veterinarian and get his opinion on the general health of the breed, as well as inquire about his experience with the breed and any problems he might have seen.

Let's assume that all of your investigations have proven fruitful. You feel sure that there's

Your carefully considered choice of the Australian Cattle Dog can result in many years of canine companionship beyond compare.

an AuCaDo puppy out there, waiting just for you, so now all you need is to find this perfect pup. Get back in touch with the breeders with whom you spoke originally and find out who has a litter of puppies. If there are none available at this time, ask questions about who's going to be breeding in the near future and when the proposed puppies will be ready to go to new homes. That, then, will become your target date and you'll use the present time to prepare yourself, your family and your home for receiving an AuCaDo puppy.

Getting a new puppy is, in many ways, a lot like having a baby. There are many things you must consider, dozens of things you must do to get ready and many arrangements that must be made for the optimum upbringing of this youngster. Let's begin by preparing yourself and your family for the new addition.

Have you thought about the fact that you'll probably have to get up earlier than usual for a while? You'll be taking the puppy out for toilet training very frequently at first. As the pup grows, he will slowly develop bladder muscle control, so the frequency and urgency of going out will subside.

Is your family willing and able to assist in the housebreaking chore? Do all of the members realize how observant they will need to be in keeping a watchful eye on the new little fellow? Are they willing to take care of scheduled feeding times? Is everyone in agreement about crate-training the puppy?

You will need to have some serious discussions about what you will and will not accept in the

---

PEDIGREE VS. REGISTRATION CERTIFICATE

Too often new owners are confused between these two important documents. Your puppy's pedigree, essentially a family tree, is a written record of a dog's genealogy of three generations or more. The pedigree will show you the names as well as performance titles of all dogs in your pup's background. Your breeder must provide you with a registration application, with his part properly filled out. You must complete the application and send it to the AKC with the proper fee. Every puppy must come from a litter that has been AKC-registered by the breeder, born in the US and from a sire and dam that are also registered with the AKC.

The seller must provide you with complete records to identify the puppy. The AKC requires that the seller provide the buyer with the following: breed; sex, color and markings; date of birth; litter number (when available); names and registration numbers of the parents; breeder's name; and date sold or delivered.

way of the puppy's behavior. For example, is the puppy going to be allowed on beds and furniture? How much freedom is the puppy going to be given once he's mature? Some families allow their dogs total freedom throughout the home, while others limit dogs to certain rooms in the house, such as the kitchen and family room. All of these things must be decided before you bring the puppy into your home.

Are the children going to share in exercising the pup? If you have very small children, are you prepared to supervise the kids as well as the dog? Are you aware of how important it is that children and dogs should never be left alone at anytime without adult supervision? Mistakes can happen and dogs don't always understand the behavior of little ones, so protect your children and your puppy by always being there

Quality pups begin with a quality breeding program. Here is Aust. Ch. Meroolestate Kristie with her two-week-old pups. Owned by Narelle Robertson.

"YOU BETTER SHOP AROUND!"
Finding a reputable breeder who sells healthy pups is very important, but make sure that the breeder you choose is not only someone you respect but also someone with whom you feel comfortable. Your breeder will be a resource long after you buy your puppy, and you must be able to call with reasonable questions without being made to feel like a pest! If you don't connect on a personal level, investigate some other breeders before making a final decision.

when they are together.

Now, about your home. Is it prepared to weather the effects of a growing puppy? Have you purchased baby gates to close off certain spaces in the house where you can keep the puppy safe from harm and the house safe from the curious puppy? Blocking off stairways is another important factor. The puppy can be taught to safely negotiate stairs, but it will take a little while and you won't want your puppy to get hurt before he learns how to manage them.

If you have a yard, the puppy can be allowed to play there, providing it is fenced. The fence should be about 4 feet high and totally secure, without holes or small escape spots. Do not leave the puppy in the yard without your supervision, as he can get into all sorts of trouble when you're not watching him.

All electrical cords and other wires, such as those for the TV, VCR and telephone, must be kept out of puppy's reach. Given the opportunity, the pup is likely to find them fascinating and fun to chew on. Knickknacks and small items on low tables are an invitation to grab and chew. So are shoes left out and around. Trash bins smell inviting to dogs, and puppies love to tip them over and investigate their contents. You will need to be certain that all wastebaskets are placed out of puppy's reach before he arrives home.

Make arrangements to have a veterinarian see your puppy within a week or so of his arrival home. Having a veterinarian that you trust and respect will be key to maintaining your dog's health for his entire life. The vet should be well-known in your community and admired by other dog owners with whom you've consulted regarding their pets' health care.

At the initial meeting with your proposed veterinarian, he will check the puppy's previous shot record and administer whatever immunization shots are required at that time. Find out how the vet can be reached at night and on weekends when the office is closed. If an emergency

TEMPERAMENT COUNTS
Your selection of a good puppy can be determined by your needs. A show or working potential or a good pet? It is your choice. Every puppy, however, should be of good temperament. Although show-quality puppies are bred and raised with emphasis on physical conformation, responsible breeders strive for equally good temperament. Do not buy from a breeder who concentrates solely on physical traits at the expense of temperamental soundness.

arises, the last thing you want to do is have to search for someone to care for your dog. Keep telephone numbers and names in a handy place where all family members can find them quickly.

While you're waiting for your target date to arrive, in addition to all of these preparations, another important decision must be made. You need to decide whether you want a female or a male puppy. Once you've made up your mind, it's prudent to call the breeder and let him know your choice. If you're still not sure or have no preference, you can simply make your choice when you visit the litter. Usually breeders will let you see the pups a few weeks before they are ready to leave, and you can make your selection at that time. Maybe you'll see one particular puppy whose behavior just speaks to you. The puppy seems to be saying, "Take me!" Many dog owners claim they didn't pick their puppy—their puppy picked them!

Males are frequently more independent than females, though just as loving toward their owners. Adult intact males can be more dominant and often resent the presence of other males in their territory. To prevent aggressive behavior problems in adult males, this trait must be curbed

In a working breed like the AuCaDo, color is not a major concern and is a matter of personal preference when choosing a dog. Both Cattle Dog colorations are equally striking.

> **BOY OR GIRL?**
> An important consideration to be discussed is the sex of your puppy. For a family companion, a bitch may be the better choice, considering the female's inbred concern for all young creatures and her accompanying tolerance and patience. It is always advisable to spay a pet bitch or neuter a pet male, which may guarantee your dog a longer life.

when the dog is a puppy. A course in basic obedience can serve to teach the dog self-control and, in addition, to teach the dog what is and what is not acceptable behavior. Males are wonderful companions that demonstrate their love through their devotion to their family.

Females are usually more docile and quiet than males, though just as loving and devoted to their owners. Except when they are in season, they tend to stay closer to home and lack the instinct to wander. Once in heat, however, the female may run off if given the opportunity to search for available males for mating. Occasionally a female may be snappish during her heat cycle, so the owner will need to be careful with her around strangers at that time. For the person simply wanting a companion or helper, rather than a potential show or breeding dog, a neutered male or

spayed female is obviously preferable to a sexually intact one.

Whatever your decision, you should plan right from the start to neuter or spay your pet puppy at the appropriate time to assure you have the best possible relationship with your dog. In addition, altered dogs, both male and female, are at a much lower risk for cancer than intact dogs. Neutering males helps them settle into their homes and not become neighborhood nuisances with wandering. Without the production of hormones, the male dog lacks the desire to breed, making him a more reliable and easygoing companion. Likewise, spaying females is definitely a must. Females come into season twice a year and the heat cycles last for about 21 days, during which time they attract males from miles around. Having a group of males parked in your front yard for three weeks and ruining your flowers and shrubs with urine is enough to convince you to spay, not to mention the accompanying health benefits for your dog.

Before your new puppy arrives, do some research into the availability of puppy training classes in your area. Often called Kindergarten Puppy Training classes, they specialize in socializing your puppy with other puppies and their owners. The puppies are taught simple basic obedience behaviors such as sit,

ARE YOU PREPARED?
Unfortunately, when a puppy is bought by someone who does not take into consideration the time and attention that dog ownership requires, it is the puppy who suffers when he is either abandoned or placed in a shelter by a frustrated owner. So all of the "homework" you do in preparation for your pup's arrival will benefit you both. The more informed you are, the more you will know what to expect and the better equipped you will be to handle the ups and downs of raising a puppy. Hopefully, everyone in the household is willing to do his part in raising and caring for the pup. The anticipation of owning a dog often brings a lot of promises from excited family members: "I will walk him every day," "I will feed him," "I will house-train him," etc., but these things take time and effort, and promises can easily be forgotten once the novelty of the new pet has worn off.

down, come and heel (how to walk nicely without pulling their owners down the street). People who have experienced a puppy class often comment that it was fascinating and fun to watch all of the puppies grow and develop into pleasant, willing companions. The normal eight-week course should be well worth the price and effort for all concerned.

Once the puppy reaches the age of about eight months, he can be considered an adult, although he probably won't fill out and look mature until around one year of age. During the adolescent period of five to eight months, the puppy can be enrolled in a basic beginner obedience class rather than the puppy class. Regardless, your new pup will need some form of basic training to teach him manners and self-control.

The "big day" is getting close. When the much-anticipated litter

If you aspire to show, be sure to make your intentions clear to the breeder. This future star is already practicing his pose!

> **PET INSURANCE**
> Just like you can insure your car, your house and your own health, you likewise can insure your dog's health. Investigate a pet insurance policy by talking to your vet. Depending on the age of your dog, the breed and the kind of coverage you desire, your policy can be very affordable. Most policies cover accidental injuries, poisoning and thousands of medical problems and illnesses, including cancers. Some carriers also offer routine care and immunization coverage.

reaches six weeks of age, it's time to visit them. The average AuCaDo litter is four to six puppies, and you'll surely enjoy watching the siblings interact with each other! You also should meet the dam (mother) and sire (father), if he is on the premises, and observe the puppies as they interact with their parent(s). If possible, get to know the parent dogs and observe their temperaments. Are they friendly? Calm and confident? Good with the puppies?

Pay close attention to the environment in which the dogs live. Does the home look and smell clean? Is it a safe place, free of dangerous obstacles and potential problems that the puppies can get into? Is the atmosphere pleasant and free of loud noises and irritating distractions?

Next, observe the puppies as they interact with the breeder, with you and with other dogs in the home. You won't want to choose a puppy that's fearful or so subdued that he doesn't react favorably to his environment. Rather, look for puppies that are delighted to see the breeder as he enters the room. Ideally, you'll be looking for puppies that are curious about you and, by their actions, show that they're eager to make friends. Regardless of a breed's ideal temperament at maturity, all puppies are usually curious and friendly. If possible, sit down with them and let them investigate you and your smells. Let them crawl into your lap, lick your hands and otherwise show by their behavior that they want to be friends.

Other dogs in the home should be tolerant of the baby dogs and, even if they're not the puppies' parents, be gentle and

Observe the breeder with all of her dogs, not just the litter. The dogs should be good-tempered and affectionate toward their owner, signs of good breeding and proper care.

non-aggressive. Many times an adult dog will tire of the puppies' antics and quietly turn away from them rather than put up with their clamoring and nipping.

Now is the ideal time to inform the breeder about your decision concerning your preferred gender. Also discuss the approximate date when the puppies will be ready to go to their new homes. Set aside a date and time when you will return to pick up your puppy.

PUPPY APPEARANCE

Your puppy should have a well-fed appearance but not a distended abdomen, which may indicate worms or incorrect feeding, or both. The body should be firm, with a solid feel. The skin of the abdomen should be pale pink and clean, without signs of scratching or rash. Check the legs to see if the dewclaws have been removed, as this is done at just a few weeks old.

Ask about a sales contract, health guarantee and the puppy's papers (registration certificate and pedigree). The breeder can explain about each of these to you. Now also is the time to get feeding instructions from the

INHERIT THE MIND
In order to know whether or not a puppy will fit into your lifestyle, you need to assess his personality. A good way to do this is to interact with his parents. Your pup inherits not only his appearance but also his personality and temperament from the sire and dam. Also observe any other adult dogs on the breeder's premises, as these will give you an idea of how dogs of the breeder's line mature.

breeder. Find out what brand of dog food the pups are eating and the amount and times when they're fed. You should duplicate this schedule as closely as possible for the first few weeks after bringing your puppy into his new home. If you choose later to change the puppy's diet, consult your veterinarian before doing so.

Finally, there's one more element of this puppy-choosing business that we need to discuss. That is the mysterious matter of seeing a puppy pick his new owner. It doesn't happen often, but, when it does, there is no doubt in anyone's mind that this is a case of unexplainable attraction that cannot be denied.

Several years ago, I went with a friend to pick out a puppy from a large litter of Standard Poodle puppies. She wanted a male puppy, so I evaluated all of the males in the litter. During my time with them, my friend noticed that one particular puppy kept coming over to her and sitting down at her feet. The look on his little face clearly said, "Take me home with you."

I evaluated that particular puppy as being a "fair" prospect for her, but definitely not the best. However, as our visit progressed and the little fellow kept insisting on staying with my friend, I began to realize that he was probably going home with us.

To this day, Nemo, the

insistent little puppy that picked my friend, is still sitting beside her at every opportunity. They have trained in obedience together and Nemo often accompanies my friend to her office, where her fellow employees adore the big, black "gentleman escort." Obviously, this was a magical match created by a sensitive little puppy and a lady who wanted a companion.

This true story is a prime example of how sometimes things just work out for the best and a perfect match is created. My friend had done her homework and she knew what she wanted, yet she was open to other possibilities. And when one particular puppy made his feelings known, she heeded his call and responded in kind.

Selecting your puppy will be an adventure for you and your whole family. Of course, if you have chosen a good breeder, he will be a wonderful source of information and guidance regarding the breed and which puppy in the litter will suit you

As pretty as a picture, this AuCaDo youngster exemplifies the look of health and alertness that new owners seek.

and your family best. Likewise, if you plan to show or work your AuCaDo, the breeder can guide you to the pups with the most potential in those aspects. If, however, you can't find the puppy that's right for you, be patient. In due time, the perfect pup will emerge and you'll have a friend for life. It'll be worth the wait.

COMMITMENT OF OWNERSHIP
You have chosen the Australian Cattle Dog, which means that you have decided which characteristics you want in a dog and what type of dog will best fit into your family and lifestyle. If you have selected a breeder, you have gone a step further—you have done your research and found a responsible, conscientious person who

A HEALTHY PUP
You should not even think about buying a puppy that looks sick, undernourished, overly frightened or nervous. Sometimes a timid puppy will warm up to you after a 30-minute "let's-get-acquainted" session.

HEALTHY AND HAPPY
Choosing a puppy with sparkling eyes and a bright expression is sure to get you a dog that's intelligent and curious. Also, a well-formed, solid stool usually means a healthy pup. Loose stool can be a sign of trouble such as a digestive or stomach problem.

breeds quality Australian Cattle Dogs and who should be a reliable source of help as you and your puppy adjust to life together. If you have observed a litter in action, you have obtained a firsthand look at the dynamics of a puppy "pack" and, thus, you have learned about each pup's individual personality—perhaps you have even found one that particularly appeals to you.

Researching your breed, selecting a responsible breeder and observing as many pups as possible are all important steps on the way to dog ownership. It may seem like a lot of effort...and you have not even taken the pup home yet! Remember, though, you cannot be too careful when it comes to deciding on the type of dog you want and finding out about your prospective pup's background. Buying a puppy is not—or *should* not be—just another whimsical purchase. This is one instance in which you actually do get to choose your own family!

You may be thinking that buying a puppy should be fun—it should not be so serious and so much work. Keep in mind that your puppy is not a cuddly stuffed toy or decorative lawn ornament; rather, he is a living creature that will become a real member of your family. You will come to realize that, while buying a puppy is a pleasurable and exciting endeavor, it is not something to be taken lightly. Relax...the fun will start when the pup comes home!

Always keep in mind that a puppy is virtually helpless in a human world and trusts his owner for fulfillment of his basic needs for survival. In addition to food, water and shelter, your pup needs care, protection, guidance and love. If you are not prepared to commit to this, then you are not prepared to own a dog.

"Wait a minute," you say. "How hard could this be? All of my neighbors own dogs and they seem to be doing just fine. Why should I have to worry about all of this?" Well, you should not worry about it; in fact, you will probably find that once your AuCaDo pup gets used to his new home, he will fall into his place in the family quite naturally. However, it never hurts to emphasize the commitment of dog ownership. With some time and patience, it is really not too difficult to raise a curious and

PUPPY PERSONALITY
When a litter becomes available to you, choosing a pup out of all those adorable faces will not be an easy task! Sound temperament is of utmost importance, but each pup has its own personality and some may be better suited to you than others. A feisty, independent pup will do well in a home with older children and adults, while quiet, shy puppies will thrive in homes with minimal noise and distractions. Your breeder knows the pups best and should be able to guide you in the right direction.

exuberant Australian Cattle Dog pup to be a well-adjusted and well-mannered adult dog—a dog that could be your most loyal friend.

PREPARING PUPPY'S PLACE IN YOUR HOME

As discussed, you will have to prepare your home and family beforehand for the new addition. Much as you would prepare a nursery for a newborn baby, you will need to designate a place in your home that will be the puppy's own. How you prepare your home will depend on how much freedom the dog will be allowed. Whatever you decide,

It's easy to be bowled over by the Cattle Dog!

Your pet shop should have a variety of crates to choose from. Select a sturdy crate that will comfortably house your AuCaDo at his adult size.

PHOTO COURTESY OF DOSKOCIL.

of his mother and littermates, as well as the familiarity of the only place he has ever known, so it is important to make his transition as easy as possible. By preparing a place in your home for the puppy, you are making him feel as welcome as possible in a strange new place. It should not take him long to get used to it, but the sudden shock of being trans-planted is somewhat traumatic for a young pup. Imagine how a small child would feel in the same situation—that is how your puppy must be feeling. It is up to you to reassure him and to let him know, "Little heeler, you are going to like it here!"

WHAT YOU SHOULD BUY

CRATE

To someone unfamiliar with the use of crates in dog training, it may seem like punishment to shut a dog in a crate, but this is not the case at all. More and more breeders and trainers around the world are recommending crates as preferred tools for pet puppies as well as show puppies.

Crates are not cruel—crates have many humane and highly effective uses in dog care and training. For example, crate training is a popular and very successful house-training method. In addition, a crate can keep your dog safe during travel and, perhaps most importantly, a crate

you must ensure that he has a place that he can "call his own."

When you take your new puppy into your home, you are bringing him into what will become his home as well. Obviously, you did not buy a puppy with the intentions of catering to his every whim and allowing him to "rule the roost," but in order for a puppy to grow into a stable, well-adjusted dog, he has to feel comfortable in his surroundings. Remember, he is leaving the warmth and security provides your dog with a place of his own in your home. It serves as a "doggie bedroom" of sorts—your AuCaDo can curl up in his crate when he wants to sleep or when he just needs a break. Many dogs sleep in their crates overnight. With soft bedding and his favorite toy, a crate becomes a cozy pseudo-den for your dog. Like his ancestors, he too will seek out the comfort and retreat of a den—you just happen to be providing him with something a little more luxurious than what his early ancestors enjoyed.

Teaching the puppy to enjoy his crate will give him a feeling of security. In addition, you will know that he is safe and out of harm's way while your house is safe from a chewing puppy. Remember that all puppies chew, and having a crate-trained puppy keeps everyone and everything safe from those sharp little teeth.

As far as purchasing a crate, the type that you buy is up to you. It will most likely be one of the two most popular types: wire or fiberglass. There are advantages and disadvantages to each type. For example, a wire crate is more open, allowing the air to flow through and affording the dog a view of what is going on around him, while a fiberglass crate is sturdier. Both can double as travel crates, providing protection for the dog in the car.

The size of the crate is another thing to consider. The

A crate is necessary for many reasons, including safe travel. Accustoming your pup to a crate in the home means that he will be able to accept the crate in other situations when needed.

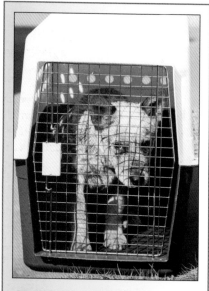

CRATE-TRAINING TIPS

During crate training, you should partition off the section of the crate in which the pup stays. If he is given too big an area, this will hinder your training efforts. Crate training is based on the fact that a dog does not like to soil his sleeping quarters, so it is ineffective to keep a pup in an area that is so big that he can eliminate in one end and get far enough away from it to sleep. Also, you want to make the crate den-like for the pup. Blankets and a favorite toy will make the crate cozy for the small pup; as he grows, you may want to evict some of his "roommates" to make more room. It will take some coaxing at first, but be patient. Given some time to get used to it, your pup will adapt to his new-home-within-a-home quite nicely.

crate should be big enough for the dog to lie down and stretch out his legs and stand up without hitting his head on the top. When purchasing a crate for a puppy, choose one that will fit the dog as an adult; do not use his puppy size as a guide. While a small crate may be fine for a very young AuCaDo pup, it will not do him much good for long! Unless you have the money and the inclination to buy a new crate every time your pup has a growth spurt, it is better to get one right from the start that will accommodate your dog both as a pup and at full size. A medium-sized crate will be necessary for a full-grown Australian Cattle Dog, who can stand up to 20 inches high at the shoulder.

BEDDING

A soft lambswool pad in the dog's crate will help the dog feel more at home, and you may also like to give him a small blanket. First, these things will take the place of the leaves, twigs, etc. that the pup would use in the wild to make a den; the pup can make his own "burrow" in the crate. Although your pup is far removed from his den-making ancestors, the denning instinct is still a part of his genetic makeup. Second, until you take your pup home, he has been sleeping amid the warmth of his dam and littermates, and while a blanket is not the same as a warm, breathing body, it still provides heat and something with which to snuggle. You will want to wash your pup's bedding frequently in case he has a potty accident in his crate, and replace or remove any blanket or padding that becomes ragged and starts to fall apart.

TOYS

Toys are a must for dogs of all ages, especially for curious playful pups. Puppies are the "children" of the dog world, and what child does not love toys? Chew toys provide enjoyment for both dog and owner—your dog will enjoy playing with his favorite toys, while you will enjoy the fact that they distract him from chewing on your expensive shoes and leather sofa. Puppies love to chew; in fact, chewing is a physical need for pups as they are teething, and everything looks appetizing! The full range of your possessions—from old dish rag to Oriental carpet—are fair game in the eyes of a teething pup. Puppies are not all that discerning when it comes to finding something literally to "sink their teeth into"—everything tastes great!

Australian Cattle Dog puppies are fairly aggressive chewers and only the hardest, strongest toys should be offered to them. Remember, you'd rather that your pup uses his teeth on safe toys

DEALING WITH FEAR

Puppies can experience a "fear period" around the age of eight weeks. The period can last for 30 minutes, for a day or even for a week. For example, the vacuum cleaner is sitting in the middle of the floor when suddenly the pup shies away from it and won't enter the room. The vacuum cleaner has been there many times and the pup has never before shown concern about it. However, on this day, he's petrified of it.

Ignore the matter, go about your business as if nothing has happened and do not encourage the pup to get near the machine. In a short time, the pup will once again ignore the vacuum cleaner and you'll be left wondering if the whole episode was a dream. It was merely a short fear period during which the puppy became afraid of a common item that he usually sees every day. Ignoring the episode will help it pass quickly.

Too much attention to the puppy regarding the matter may prolong the fear period and encourage the pup to keep being afraid just to get your attention. This whole fear period scenario may repeat itself when the puppy is about eight months old. Treat it the same way as before and it will soon pass.

than on your heels! Breeders advise owners to resist stuffed toys, because they can become de-stuffed in no time. The overly

A sturdy, lightweight nylon lead will be suitable for your AuCaDo puppy, but you will need to purchase stronger leads as the dog grows in size and strength.

TOYS, TOYS, TOYS!

With a big variety of dog toys available, and so many that look like they would be a lot of fun for a dog, be careful in your selection. It is amazing what a set of puppy teeth can do to an innocent-looking toy, so, obviously, safety is a major consideration. Be sure to choose the most durable products that you can find. Hard nylon bones and toys are a safe bet, and many of them are offered in different scents and flavors that will be sure to capture your dog's attention. It is always fun to play a game of fetch with your dog, and there are balls and flying discs that are specially made to withstand dog teeth.

excited pup may ingest the stuffing, which is neither nutritious nor digestible.

Similarly, squeaky toys are quite popular, but must be avoided for the AuCaDo. Perhaps a squeaky toy can be used as an aid in training, but not for free play. If a pup "disembowels" one of these, the small plastic squeaker inside can be dangerous if swallowed. Monitor the condition of all your pup's toys carefully and get rid of any that have been chewed to the point of becoming potentially dangerous.

Be careful of natural bones, which have a tendency to splinter into sharp, dangerous pieces. Also be careful of rawhide, which can turn into pieces that are easy to swallow and become a mushy mess on your carpet.

LEAD

A nylon lead is probably the best option, as it is the most resistant to puppy teeth should your pup take a liking to chewing on his lead. Of course, this is a habit that should be nipped in the bud, but, if your pup likes to chew on his lead, he has a very slim chance of being able to chew through the strong nylon. Nylon leads are also lightweight, which is good for a young AuCaDo who is just getting used to the idea of walking on a lead. For everyday walking and safety purposes, the nylon lead is a good choice.

As your pup grows up and gets used to walking on the lead, and can do it politely, you may want to purchase a flexible lead. These leads allow you to extend the length to give the dog a broader area to explore or to shorten the length to keep the dog near you.

COLLAR

Your pup should get used to wearing a collar all the time since you will want to attach his ID tags to it; plus, you have to attach the lead to something! A lightweight nylon collar is a good choice. Make certain that the collar fits snugly enough so that the pup cannot wriggle out of it, but is loose enough so that it will not be uncomfortably tight around the pup's neck. You should be able to fit a finger between the pup's neck and the collar. It may take some time for your pup to get used to wearing the collar, but soon he

Your local pet shop should have a wide selection of food and water bowls. Purchase sturdy "chew-proof" bowls that can be cleaned easily.

PHOTO COURTESY OF MIKKI PET PRODUCTS.

CHOOSE AN APPROPRIATE COLLAR

The **BUCKLE COLLAR** is the standard collar used for everyday purposes. Be sure that you adjust the buckle on growing puppies. Check it every day. It can become too tight overnight! These collars can be made of leather or nylon. Attach your dog's identification tags to this collar.

The **CHOKE COLLAR** is designed for training. It is constructed of highly polished steel so that it slides easily through the stainless steel loop. The idea is that the dog controls the pressure around his neck and he will stop pulling if the collar becomes uncomfortable. It is used *only* during training and *never* left on a dog.

The **HALTER** is for a trained dog that has to be restrained to prevent running away, chasing a cat and the like. Considered the most humane of all collars, it is frequently used on smaller dogs on which collars are not comfortable.

will not even notice that it is there. The choke collar is made for use during training, but should only be used by an owner who has been instructed in its proper use.

FOOD AND WATER BOWLS

Your pup will need two bowls, one for food and one for water. You may want two sets of bowls, one for indoors and one for outdoors, depending on where the dog will be fed and where he will be spending time. Stainless steel or sturdy plastic bowls are popular choices. Plastic bowls are more chewable, but dogs tend not to chew on the steel variety, which can be sterilized. It is important to buy sturdy bowls since anything is in danger of being chewed by puppy teeth and you do not want your dog to be constantly chewing apart his bowl (for his safety and for your wallet!).

CLEANING SUPPLIES

Until a pup is house-trained, you will be doing a lot of cleaning. "Accidents" will occur, which is acceptable in the beginning stages of toilet training because the puppy does not know any better. All you can do is be prepared to clean up any accidents as soon as they happen. Old towels, paper towels, newspapers and a safe disinfectant are good to have on hand.

NATURAL TOXINS

Examine your grass and landscaping before bringing your puppy home. Many varieties of plants have leaves, stems or flowers that are toxic if ingested, and you can depend on a curious puppy to investigate them.

If you see your dog carrying a piece of vegetation in his mouth, approach him in a quiet, disinterested manner, avoid eye contact, pet him and gradually remove the plant from his mouth. Alternatively, offer him a treat and maybe he'll drop the plant on his own accord. Be sure no toxic plants are growing in your own yard or kept in your home. Ask your vet for information on poisonous plants or research them at your library.

BEYOND THE BASICS

The items previously discussed are the bare necessities. You will find out what else you need as you go along—grooming supplies, flea/tick protection, baby gates to partition a room, etc. These things

Your Cattle Dog puppy will be quick to "dig in" to exploring his new surroundings, so be sure to keep an eye on him and to provide a puppy-proof area in which he can roam.

will vary depending on your situation, but it is important that you have everything you need to feed and make your Australian Cattle Dog comfortable in his first few days at home.

PUPPY-PROOFING YOUR HOME

Aside from making sure that your AuCaDo will be comfortable in your home, you also have to make sure that your home is safe for your AuCaDo. This means taking precautions that your pup will not get into anything he should not get into and that there is nothing within his reach that may harm him should he sniff it, chew it, inspect it, etc. This probably seems obvious since, while you are primarily concerned with your pup's safety, at the same time you

do not want your belongings to be ruined. Breakables should be placed out of reach if your dog is to have full run of the house. If he is to be limited to certain places within the house, keep any potentially dangerous items in the "off-limits" areas.

As we've mentioned, an electrical cord can pose a danger should the puppy decide to taste it—and who is going to convince a pup that it would not make a great chew toy? Cords and wires should be fastened tightly against the wall, out of puppy's sight and away from his teeth. If your dog is going to spend time in a crate, make sure that there is nothing near his crate that he can reach if he sticks his curious little nose or paws through the openings. Just as you would with a child, keep all household cleaners and chemicals where the pup cannot reach them.

It is also important to make sure that the outside of your home is safe. Of course, your puppy should never be unsupervised, but a pup let loose in the yard will want to run and explore, and he should be granted that freedom. Do not let a fence give you a false sense of security; you would be surprised at how crafty (and persistent) a dog can be in figuring out how to dig under and squeeze his way through small holes, or to jump or climb over a fence. The remedy is to make the fence well embedded into the ground and high enough so that it really is impossible for your dog to get over it (a fence of at least 4 feet should suffice). Be sure to secure any gaps in the fence. Check the fence periodically to ensure that it is in good shape and make repairs as needed; a very determined pup may return to the same spot to "work on it" until he is able to get through.

FIRST TRIP TO THE VET

You have selected your puppy, and your home and family are ready. Now all you have to do is collect your AuCaDo from the breeder and the fun begins, right? Well…not so fast. Something else you need to plan is your pup's first trip to the veterinarian. Perhaps the breeder can recommend someone in the area who specializes in the breed, or maybe you know some other Australian Cattle Dog owners who can suggest a good vet. Either way, you should have an appointment arranged for your pup before you pick him up.

The pup's first visit will consist of an overall examination to make sure that the pup does not have any problems that are not apparent to you. The veterinarian will also set up a schedule for the pup's vaccinations; the breeder will inform you of which ones the pup has already received and the vet can continue from there.

CHEMICAL TOXINS
Scour your garage for potential puppy dangers. Remove weed killers, pesticides and antifreeze materials. Antifreeze is highly toxic and just a few drops can kill a puppy or an adult dog. The sweet taste attracts the animal, who will quickly consume it from the floor or pavement.

INTRODUCTION TO THE FAMILY

Everyone in the house will be excited about the puppy's coming home and will want to pet him and play with him, but it is best to make the introductions low-key so as not to overwhelm the puppy. He is apprehensive already. It is the first time he has been separated from his mother and the breeder, and the ride to your home is likely to be the first time he has been in a car. The last thing you want to do is smother him, as this will only frighten him

What an exciting day for the whole family when it comes time to bring home the new Australian Cattle Dog puppy!

IN DUE TIME

It will take at least two weeks for your puppy to become accustomed to his new surroundings. Give him lots of love, attention, handling, frequent opportunities to relieve himself, a diet he likes to eat and a place he can call his own.

further. This is not to say that human contact is not extremely necessary at this stage, because this is the time when a connection between the pup and his human family is formed. Gentle petting and soothing words should help console him, as well as just putting him down and letting him explore on his own (under your watchful eye, of course).

The pup may approach the family members or may busy himself with exploring for a while. Gradually, each person should spend some time with the pup, one at a time, crouching down to get as close to the pup's level as possible while letting him sniff each person's hands and petting him gently. He definitely needs human attention and he needs to be touched—this is how to form an immediate bond. Just remember that the pup is experiencing many things for the first time, at the same time. There are new people, new noises, new smells and new things to investigate, so be gentle, be affectionate and be as comforting as you can be.

PUP'S FIRST NIGHT HOME

You have traveled home with your new charge safely in his crate. He's been to the vet for a thorough check-up; he's been weighed, his papers have been examined and perhaps he's even been vaccinated and wormed as well. He's met the whole family, including the excited children and the less-than-happy cat. He's explored his area, his new bed, the yard and anywhere else he's been permitted. He's eaten his first meal at home and relieved himself in the proper place. He's heard lots of new sounds, smelled new friends and seen more of the outside world than ever before...and that was just the first day! He's worn out and is ready for bed...or so you think!

It's puppy's first night home and you are ready to say "Good night." Keep in mind that this is his first night ever to be sleeping alone. His dam and littermates are no longer at paw's length and he's a bit scared, cold and lonely. Be reassuring to your new family member, but this is not the time to spoil him and give in to his inevitable whining.

Puppies whine. They whine to let others know where they are and hopefully to get company out of it. Place your pup in his new bed or crate in his designated area and close the crate door. Mercifully, he may fall asleep without a peep. When the inevitable occurs, however, ignore the whining—he is fine. Be strong and keep his interest in mind. Do not allow yourself to feel guilty and visit the pup. He will fall asleep eventually.

Many breeders recommend placing a piece of bedding from the pup's former home in his new bed so that he recognizes and is comforted by the scent of his littermates. Others still advise placing a hot water bottle in the bed for warmth. The latter may be a good idea provided the pup doesn't attempt to suckle—he'll get good and wet, and may not fall asleep so fast.

Puppy's first night can be somewhat stressful for both the pup and his new family. Remember that you are setting the tone of nighttime at your house. Unless you want to play with your pup every night at 10 p.m., midnight and 2 a.m., don't initiate the habit. Your family will thank you, and soon so will your pup!

MANNERS MATTER

During the socialization process, a puppy should meet people, experience different environments and definitely be exposed to other canines. Through playing and interacting with other dogs, your puppy will learn lessons, ranging from controlling the pressure of his jaws by biting his littermates to the inner-workings of the canine pack that he will apply to his human relationships for the rest of his life. That is why removing a puppy from the litter too early (before eight weeks) can be detrimental to the pup's development.

PROPER SOCIALIZATION

The socialization period for puppies is from age 8 to 16 weeks. This is the time when puppies need to leave their birth family and take up residence with their new owners, where they will meet many new people, other pets, etc. Failure to be adequately socialized can cause the dog to grow up fearing others and being shy and unfriendly due to a lack of self-confidence.

PREVENTING PUPPY PROBLEMS

SOCIALIZATION

Now that you have done all of the preparatory work and have helped your pup get accustomed to his new home and family, it is about time for you to have some fun! Socializing your Australian Cattle Dog pup gives you the opportunity to show off your new friend, and your pup gets to reap the benefits of being an adorable intriguing creature that people will want to pet and, in general, think is absolutely precious!

Besides getting to know his new family, your puppy should be exposed to other people, animals and situations. This will help him become well adjusted as he grows up and less prone to being timid or fearful of the new things he will encounter. Of course, he must not come into close contact with dogs you don't know well until his course of injections is fully complete.

Your pup's socialization began with the breeder, but now it is your responsibility to continue it. The socialization he receives until the age of 12 weeks is the most critical, as this is the time when he forms his impressions of the outside world. Be especially careful during the eight-to-ten-week-old period, also known as the fear period. The interaction he receives during this time should be gentle and reassuring. Lack of socialization, and/or negative experiences during the socialization period, can manifest itself in fear and aggression as the dog grows up. Your puppy needs lots of positive interaction, which of course includes human contact, affection, handling and exposure to other animals.

Once your pup has received his necessary vaccinations, feel free to take him out and about (on his lead, of course). Walk him around the neighborhood, take

PUP MEETS WORLD

Thorough socialization includes not only meeting new people but also being introduced to new experiences such as riding in the car, having his coat brushed, hearing the television, walking in a crowd—the list is endless. The more your pup experiences, and the more positive the experiences are, the less of a shock and the less frightening it will be for your pup to encounter new things.

him on your daily errands, let people pet him, let him meet other dogs and pets, etc. Puppies do not have to try to make friends; there will be no shortage of people who will want to introduce themselves. Just make sure that you carefully supervise each meeting. If the neighborhood children want to say hello, for example, that is great—children and pups most often make great companions. However, sometimes an excited child can unintentionally handle a pup too roughly, or an overzealous pup can playfully nip a little too hard. You want to make socialization experiences positive ones. What a pup learns during this very formative stage will affect his attitude toward future encounters. You want your dog to be comfortable around everyone. A pup that has a bad

experience with a child may grow up to be a dog that is shy around or aggressive toward children.

CONSISTENCY IN TRAINING

Dogs, being pack animals, naturally need a leader, or else they try to establish dominance in their packs. When you welcome a dog into your family, the choice of who becomes the leader and who becomes the "pack" is entirely up to you! Your pup's intuitive quest for dominance, coupled with the fact that it is nearly impossible to look at an adorable AuCaDo's "puppy-dog" face and not cave in, give the pup almost an unfair advantage in getting the upper hand!

A pup will definitely test the waters to see what he can and cannot do. Do not give in to those pleading eyes—stand your ground when it comes to disciplining the pup and make sure that all family members do the same. It will only confuse the pup if Mother tells

Not all dog/cat relationships become this cozy, but Cattle Dogs can be friends with other pets in the home, given proper introductions and time to get to know each other.

CHEWING TIPS

Chewing goes hand in hand with nipping in the sense that a teething puppy is always looking for a way to soothe his aching gums. In this case, instead of chewing on you, he may have taken a liking to your favorite shoe or something else that he should not be chewing. Again, realize that this is a normal canine behavior that does not need to be discouraged, only redirected. Your pup just needs to be taught what is acceptable to chew on and what is off-limits. Consistently tell him "No!" when you catch him chewing on something forbidden and give him a chew toy.

Conversely, praise him when you catch him chewing on something appropriate. In this way, you are discouraging the inappropriate behavior and reinforcing the desired behavior. The puppy's chewing should stop after his adult teeth have come in, but an adult dog continues to chew for various reasons—perhaps because he is bored, needs to relieve tension or just likes to chew. That is why it is important to redirect his chewing when he is still young.

him to get off the sofa when he is used to sitting up there with Father to watch the nightly news. Avoid discrepancies by having all members of the household decide on the rules before the pup even comes home…and be consistent in enforcing them! Early training shapes the dog's personality, so you cannot be unclear in what you expect.

COMMON PUPPY PROBLEMS

The best way to prevent puppy problems is to be proactive in stopping an undesirable behavior as soon as it starts. The old saying "You can't teach an old dog new tricks" does not necessarily hold true, but it *is* true that it is much easier to discourage bad behavior in a young developing pup than to wait until the pup's bad behavior becomes the adult dog's bad habit.

There are some problems that are especially prevalent in puppies as they develop.

Nipping

As puppies start to teethe, they feel the need to sink their teeth into anything available…unfortunately, that usually includes your fingers, arms, hair, toes…and definitely your heels! AuCaDos are bred to nip…at *cattle* not humans, though your puppy likely hasn't met a heifer so your boots will have to do. You may find this behavior cute for about a second, just until you feel how sharp those puppy teeth are. Nipping is something you want to discourage immediately and consistently with a firm "No!" (or whatever number of firm "Nos" it takes for him to understand that you mean business). Then, replace your finger with an appropriate chew toy. While this behavior is merely annoying when the dog is young, it can become dangerous as your AuCaDo's adult teeth grow in and his jaws develop if he continues to think it is okay to nip at his human friends. Your AuCaDo does not mean any harm with his bossy little nip, he's just doing what his instincts tell him. You're best to nip nipping in the bud, before he can reach your butt!

CRYING/WHINING

Your pup will often cry, whine, whimper, howl or make some type of commotion when he is left alone. This is basically his way of calling out for attention to make sure that you know he is there and that you have not forgotten about him. Your puppy feels insecure when he is left alone, when you are out of the house and he is in his crate or when you are in another part of the house and he cannot see you. The noise he is making is an expression of the anxiety he feels at being alone, so he needs to be taught that being alone is okay. You are not actually training the dog to stop making noise; rather, you are training him to feel comfortable when he is alone and thus removing the need for him to make the noise.

This is where the crate with cozy bedding and a toy comes in handy. You want to know that your pup is safe when you are not there to supervise, and you know that he will be safe in his crate rather than roaming freely about the house. In order for the pup to stay in his crate without making a fuss, he first needs to be comfortable in his crate. On that note, it is extremely important that the crate is never used as a form of punishment; this will cause the pup to view the crate as a negative place, rather than as a place of his own for safety and retreat.

Accustom the pup to the crate in short, gradually increasing time intervals in which you put him in the crate, maybe with a treat, and stay in the room with him. If he cries or makes a fuss, do not go to him, but stay in his sight. Gradually he will realize that staying in his crate is just fine without your help, and it will not be so traumatic for him when you are not around. You may want to leave the radio on softly when you leave the house; the sound of human voices may be comforting to him.

DEALING WITH PROBLEMS
The majority of problems that are commonly seen in young pups will disappear as your dog gets older. However, how you deal with problems when he is young will determine how he reacts to discipline as an adult dog. It is important to establish who is boss (ideally it will be you!) right away when you are first bonding with your dog. This bond will set the tone for the rest of your life together.

AUSTRALIAN CATTLE DOG

By comparison with many other dog breeds, the Australian Cattle Dog is an easy-maintenance dog. As long as you observe certain basic principles of care, your AuCaDo will be a joy to keep in top physical condition.

STORING DOG FOOD

You must store your dry dog food carefully. Open packages of dog food quickly lose their vitamin value, usually within 90 days of being opened. Mold spores and vermin could also contaminate the food.

DIETARY AND FEEDING CONSIDERATIONS

First, let's talk about feeding. The large commercial dog-food manufacturers spend millions of dollars on research to produce the optimum diet for dogs at all stages of development, from puppyhood to old age. The wise dog owner makes these products a part of his feeding plan. Puppy food, for example, is developed specifically for growing puppies.

Unless you are an expert in nutrition, concocting your own formula of meats, vegetables and supplemental herbs, vitamins and minerals will be very time-consuming and expensive as well as likely nutritionally unbalanced for the pup. You'll raise a far healthier dog by feeding the ready-made specialty puppy foods from one of the well-known dog-food manufacturers. In addition to that, the commercial foods come ready to serve, so you'll save yourself hours of shopping and cooking a homemade mix.

If you are the type of person who enjoys giving your dog little treats occasionally, indulge yourself by giving him healthy tidbits. Your pup will learn to love your special treats and look forward to those special times when you want to reward him for good behavior. Slices of raw carrot, cut-up pieces of hotdog, bits of cooked chicken and little cubes of cheese are all tasty treats filled with extra nutrition. By the way, never give your dog chocolate, as it contains a chemical known as theobromine, which can kill the dog; onions are also toxic to dogs. Never overdo it with the treats, but an occasional bit of something the pup loves can make for a pleasant moment between you and your new puppy.

It is advisable to discuss the matter of feeding with your veterinarian at your first visit. Tell him what the breeder had been feeding, tell him what you'd like to feed the pup and ask him about the frequency of feedings and the amount of food to serve at each meal. Usually puppies under 16 weeks of age want to eat 3 times a day. After that, you can drop the midday meal and feed a meal in the morning and another at night. By the time the puppy is six months old, he should be on two meals a day.

This plan of two meals a day is an ideal routine for the rest of the dog's life. Years ago, people usually fed their dogs once a day. However, we have learned over the years that feeding a dog twice a day is better for the dog because you're not putting an excessive amount of food in the dog's stomach all at once. Besides, you're probably in the

THE FIRST WEEKS

Puppies instinctively want to suck milk from their dam's teats; a normal puppy will exhibit this behavior just a few moments following birth. If puppies do not attempt to suckle within the first half-hour or so, they should be encouraged to do so by placing them on the nipples, having selected ones with plenty of milk. This early milk supply is important in providing the essential colostrum, which protects the puppies during the first eight to ten weeks of their lives.

Although a dam's milk is much better than any commercially prepared milk formula, despite there being some excellent ones available, if the puppies do not feed, the breeder will have to feed them by hand. For those with less experience, advice from a veterinarian is important so that not only the right quantity of milk is fed but also that of correct quality, fed at suitably frequent intervals, usually every two hours during the first few days of life.

Puppies should be allowed to nurse from their dam for about the first six weeks, although, starting around the third or fourth week, the breeder will begin to introduce small portions of suitable solid food. Most breeders like to introduce alternate milk and meat meals initially, building up to weaning time.

FOOD PREFERENCE

Selecting the best dry dog food is difficult. There is no majority consensus among veterinary scientists as to the value of nutrient analysis (protein, fat, fiber, moisture, ash, cholesterol, minerals, etc.). All agree that feeding trials are what matter most, but you also have to consider the individual dog. The dog's weight, age and activity level, and what pleases his taste, all must be considered. It is probably best to take the advice of your veterinarian. Every dog has individual dietary requirements, and should be fed accordingly.

If your dog is fed a good dry food, he does not require supplements of meat or vegetables. Dogs do appreciate a little variety in their diets, so you may choose to stay with the same brand but vary the flavor. Alternatively, you may wish to add a little flavored stock to give a difference to the taste.

If you're in the process of house-training, limit the amount of water that the pup drinks after 5 p.m. so his bladder won't be full when he goes down for the night.

You'll probably notice that, once the dog reaches maturity, he will eat smaller quantities than he did when he was a puppy. That's because he's no longer growing and requires fewer calories for adult-maintenance than for puppy development. Most health-care professionals and dog-food manufacturers agree that a puppy should be fed puppy food for the first year of life. After that, he should be switched to adult food, preferably of the same brand as he had been eating in the puppy-food variety. Adult formulas are designed to maintain and nurture the active adult dog without giving him more supplements than necessary.

Ideally, he should stay on adult food until he reaches approximately seven or eight years of age. This is, however, a

Clean your dog's food bowls after each meal and change his water often. Dogs don't like dirty dishes any more than we do!

kitchen preparing your own meals in the morning and again in the evening anyway, so it's handy to feed the dog at those times. You'll find that most veterinarians approve of twice-a-day feedings as well.

Additionally, keep fresh clean water accessible to the dog at all times. If he's crate-trained, do not put water in the crate with him, but be sure he has access to it whenever he's out of his crate.

very individual matter. The older dog who still works hard every day needs a high-maintenance diet. The older dog who is no longer active around the property will not require the formula for working dogs. Thus, a senior-diet food is best for keeping him in good physical condition without loading his body with more nutrients than he requires.

Some Australian Cattle Dogs are "old" at 8 years of age, while others don't show their age until they reach 11 or 12 years. Genetics, environment, lifestyle and physical condition all contribute to determining when a dog reaches his senior years. If you're not sure about when would be appropriate to make dietary changes for your dog, check with your veterinarian about this life stage. Of course, your breeder and vet will be invaluable sources of information about your AuCaDo's diet at all stages of life.

WATER

Just as your dog needs proper nutrition from his food, water is an essential "nutrient" as well. Water keeps the dog's body properly hydrated and promotes normal function of the body's systems. We've mentioned that, during house-training, it is necessary to keep an eye on how much water your AuCaDo is drinking, but, once he is reliably

"DOES THIS COLLAR MAKE ME LOOK FAT?"

While humans may obsess about how they look and how trim their bodies are, many people believe that extra weight on their dogs is a good thing. The truth is, pets should not be over- or under-weight, as both can lead to or signal sickness. In order to tell how fit your pet is, run your hands over his ribs. Are his ribs buried under a layer of fat or are they sticking out considerably? If your pet is within his normal weight range, you should be able to feel the ribs easily, but they should not protrude abnormally. If you stand above him, the outline of his body should resemble an hourglass. Some breeds do tend to be leaner while some are a bit stockier, but making sure your dog is the right weight for his breed will certainly contribute to his good health.

A Worthy Investment

Veterinary studies have proven that a balanced high-quality diet pays off in your dog's coat quality, behavior and activity level. Invest in premium brands for the maximum payoff with your dog.

trained, he should have access to clean fresh water at all times, especially if you feed dry food only. Make certain that the dog's water bowl is clean, and change the water often.

EXERCISE

Exercise is an important issue we must address when raising a puppy. Some breeds require a minimum amount of daily exercise, such as a walk around the block. Others, such as the hunting breeds, need frequent long-range exercise to keep them in good physical and emotional condition. After all, they are bred to run for hours in pursuit of fallen game and, thus, should not tire easily.

Australian Cattle Dogs are bred to work long hours over great distances without tiring or losing their focus on the job at hand. A regimen of daily exercise is a must for AuCaDos. Even those dogs not used for working farm stock should be given much exercise and be mentally stimulated to keep them alert, well adjusted and happy. A dog whose life is a mere void, comprised of eating, sleeping and occasional stimulation, will sooner or later become a behavioral problem.

If the dog is not challenged to use his natural instincts, he will probably begin to find outlets for his talents, which are not

DO DOGS HAVE TASTE BUDS?
Watching a dog "wolf" or gobble his food, seemingly without chewing, leads an owner to wonder whether his dog can taste anything. Yes, dogs have taste buds, with sensory perception of sweet, salty and sour. Puppies are born with fully mature taste buds.

necessarily approved by the owner. Digging, chewing, barking and destroying property are all behaviors seen in frustrated dogs that do not participate in useful, structured activities. Sadly, these are the same dogs that will eventually be turned over to animal shelters for adoption. And without proper training by knowledgeable owners, the dogs frequently end up staying in shelters or, worse, being euthanized because nobody knew how to direct their energies into appropriate behaviors and they've become uncontrollable.

This whole sad scenario can be avoided by the original

Puppies get sufficient exercise just being puppies! It is never wise to overdo or force exercise with a puppy, as too-strenuous activity can damage the growing bones and joints.

owners' planning appropriate regimens of activity to stimulate and satisfy their AuCaDos' natural talents. A case in point is an AuCaDo named Cassie. Though she does not live on a farm property, she is kept busy by her owner, MaryAnn Mullen, in obedience trials, agility competition and herding trials. At six years of age, Cassie finds something stimulating to do every day of her life, and thus has no time or inclination for engaging in unwanted behaviors.

If you are contemplating becoming an AuCaDo owner, it is essential that you consider what activities you plan to provide for your dog's life-long mental and physical health. Even a person with no particular outdoor hobbies but a strong desire to own an Australian Cattle Dog can find ways to give his dog a wonderful life. Hiking is a hobby that's good for man and beast alike. It requires a minimum of equipment and can be done in both town and country, every day of the year, in all kinds of weather, alone or with other people and their dogs.

The dog and owner who walk together are healthier and happier than those who sit home and do nothing. Another, often-forgotten, aspect of hiking is the reward of meeting other people. It is one of the easiest ways to make friends and show off your dog's good manners and winning ways. Finally, a few hours spent hiking in a quiet forest can breathe renewed energy into a person whose normal life is filled with stress. Try it, you'll find it an amazing panacea that doesn't cost a cent!

GROOMING

COAT CARE

Now let's talk about grooming your AuCaDo. The fact that the breed has a short, tight coat means there will be a minimum of coat care involved. Keeping the dog clean is important, as dirt and dust accumulated in the

---

EXERCISE ALERT!

You should be careful where you exercise your dog. Many areas have been sprayed with chemicals that are highly toxic to both dogs and humans. Never allow your dog to eat grass or drink from puddles on either public or private grounds, as the run-off water may contain chemicals from sprays and herbicides.

coat can hamper the coat from protecting the dog against rain, heat, cold and foreign matter. A good brisk brushing will clean out the coat and make it shine as it makes the dog feel good to be free of foreign matter.

Bathing the AuCaDo often is not recommended. Every time you bathe a dog, the action of the shampoo removes the natural oils from the coat, thus making it easier for the coat to collect and hold foreign matter and dust. Brushing is essential; bathing is an infrequent luxury.

When your dog does require bathing—for example, let's say

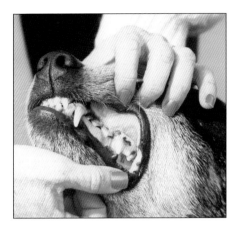

Don't forget the teeth! Dogs need dental care, too, and it's easy to incorporate routine tooth-cleaning into your grooming sessions.

he rolled in some noxious substance or got into something like a cleaning fluid that could cause skin irritation—there are a few simple steps to making the bath a pleasant event for you and your dog. Always try to bathe the dog indoors as opposed to outdoors or in a drafty location. Use warm water and a commercial dog shampoo (never a product made for human hair). Scrub vigorously to stimulate the skin and remove unwanted matter from the coat. Rinse thoroughly with warm water, then towel-dry the dog to absorb as much water as possible. Finally, let the dog stay indoors for an hour or so to allow his own body heat to complete the drying process; don't let your dog outdoors with a wet coat in cold weather.

Brushing your dog three or four times a week is an ideal plan. Dogs who live and/or work

SWEET TREATS

Giving your dog an occasional sweet treat can also be healthy for your pet. Like humans, dogs enjoy sweets and, as puppies, they quickly learn that sweet treats are very special. However, too much sugar is even worse for your dog than it is for you. To solve this dilemma, offer your dog a special treat that's healthy for him and good for his teeth. Wash and slice a carrot into quarter-inch pieces. I ask my own dog, "Do you want a penny?" and get the dog to sit before he gets his treat. That way, I'm sneaking in some training time while the dog is learning good manners. Since carrots are so sweet, your dog will love the taste while the crunchiness of the food will help polish his teeth and massage his gums.

Your local pet shop will have a variety of grooming tools. With the Cattle Dog, you will only need the basics to keep your dog's coat in proper condition.

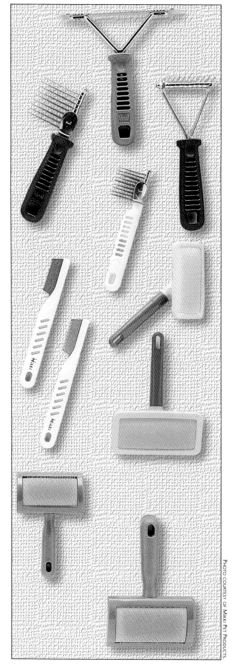

PHOTO COURTESY OF MIKKI PET PRODUCTS.

BENEFITS OF BRUSHING

Brushing your dog on a regular basis does a lot more good for the dog than just keeping the coat clean. It helps to stimulate the skin and keep the body's blood moving briskly through the dog's system. Finally, it brings natural body oils from the skin onto the hair, making the coat shine with good health.

outdoors collect all manner of foreign objects, plus dust and dirt in their coats. In addition, parasites such as fleas and ticks are periodically a problem. A frequent schedule of brushing not only will keep your dog clean but it also will help keep the dog free of unwanted parasites.

If you notice an infestation of parasites, see your veterinarian for the correct treatment to use to rid the dog of the pests. Be careful whenever you use pest-control products, as they can damage eyes, ears and noses if applied incorrectly. Finally, get advice from you vet about ridding your home and yard of those same parasites so they will not reinfest your dog. He will suggest certain products that you can purchase to use around your property.

EAR CLEANING

The ears should be kept clean with a soft wipe, such as a cotton wipe or cotton ball, and ear-cleaning

Nail Clipping

Quick

Cut Line

Nail Casing

DARK-COLORED NAIL

With black or dark nails, it's best to clip only a small bit of the nail at a time or to use a file where the quick is not visible.

LIGHT-COLORED NAIL

In light-colored nails, clipping is much simpler because you can see the vein (or quick) that grows inside the nail casing.

powder or liquid made especially for dogs. Never probe into the ear canal with a cotton swab or anything else, as this can cause injury. Be on the lookout for any signs of infection or ear-mite infestation. If your Australian Cattle Dog has been shaking his head or scratching at his ears frequently, this usually indicates a problem. If the dog's ears have an unusual odor, this is a sure sign of mite infestation or infection, and a signal to have his ears checked by the veterinarian.

Nail Clipping

Your AuCaDo should be accustomed to having his nails trimmed at an early age since nail clipping will be a part of your maintenance routine throughout his life. A dog's long nails can

Use a soft cotton wipe or ball to clean your dog's ears. Be gentle, and never probe into the ear canal.

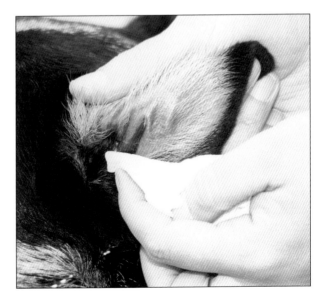

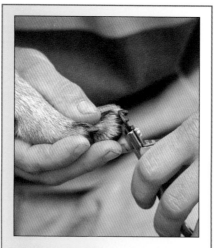

PEDICURE TIP

A dog that spends a lot of time outside on a hard surface, such as cement or pavement, will have his nails naturally worn down and may not need to have them trimmed as often, except maybe in the colder months when he is not outside as much. Regardless, it is best to get your dog accustomed to the nail-trimming procedure at an early age so that he is used to it. Some dogs are especially sensitive about having their feet touched, but if a dog has experienced it since puppyhood, it should not bother him.

Before you start cutting, make sure you can identify the "quick" in each nail. The quick is a blood vessel that runs through the center of each nail and grows rather close to the end. The quick will bleed if accidentally cut, which will be quite painful for the dog as it contains nerve endings. Keep some type of clotting agent on hand, such as a styptic pencil or styptic powder (the type used for shaving). This will stop the bleeding quickly when applied to the end of the cut nail. Do not panic if you cut the quick, just stop the bleeding and talk soothingly to your dog. Once he has calmed down, move on to the next nail. It is better to clip a little at a time, particularly with dark-nailed dogs.

Hold your pup steady as you begin trimming his nails; you do not want him to make any sudden movements or run away. Talk to him soothingly and stroke him as you clip. Holding his foot in your hand, simply take off the end of each nail with one swift clip. You should purchase nail clippers that are made for use on dogs; you can probably find them wherever you buy pet or grooming supplies.

TRAVELING WITH YOUR DOG

CAR TRAVEL

You should accustom your Australian Cattle Dog to riding in a car at an early age. You may or

scratch someone unintentionally and also have a better chance of ripping and bleeding, or causing the feet to spread. A good rule of thumb is that if you can hear your dog's nails' clicking on the floor when he walks, his nails are too long.

An AuCaDo and
his young friend
are eager to hit
the road and see
the sights.

TIPS FOR SAFE TRAVEL

Here are a few rules of the road when traveling with your dog:

- Never leave your dog alone in the car. In hot weather, your dog can die from the high temperature inside a closed vehicle; even a car parked in the shade can heat up very quickly. Leaving the window open is dangerous as well since the dog can hurt himself trying to get out.
- When you travel with your dog, it's a good idea to take along water from home or to buy bottled water for the trip. In areas where water is sometimes chemically treated and sometimes comes right out of the ground, you can prevent adverse reactions to this essential part of your dog's diet.
- When traveling, never let your dog off-lead in a strange area. Your dog could run away out of fear, decide to chase a passing squirrel or cat or simply want to stretch his legs without restriction—if any of these happen, you might never see your canine friend again.

The most extensive travel you do with your dog may be limited to trips to the vet's office—or you may decide to bring him along for long distances when the family goes on vacation. Whichever the case, it is important to consider your dog's safety while traveling.

may not take him in the car often, but at the very least he will need to go to the vet and you do not want these trips to be traumatic for the dog or troublesome for you. The safest way for a dog to ride in the car is in his crate. If he uses a crate in the house, you can use the same crate for travel.

Put the pup in the crate and see how he reacts. If he seems uneasy, you can have a passenger hold him on his lap while you drive. Another option for car travel is a specially made safety harness for dogs, which straps the dog in much like a seat belt. Whatever option you choose, do not let the dog roam loose in the vehicle—this is very dangerous! If you should stop short, your dog can be thrown and injured. If the dog starts climbing on you and pestering you while you are driving, you will not be able to concentrate on the road. It is an unsafe situation for everyone— human and canine.

For long trips, be prepared to stop to let the dog relieve himself. Take with you whatever you need to clean up after him, including some paper towels and perhaps some old rags for use should he have a potty accident in the car or suffer from motion sickness.

AIR TRAVEL

Contact your chosen airline before proceeding with your travel plans that include your Australian Cattle Dog. The dog will be required to travel in a fiberglass crate and you should always check in advance with the airline regarding specific requirements for the crate's size, type and labeling, as well as any travel restrictions and health certificates needed for the dog.

To help put your AuCaDo at ease for the trip, be sure he is well acclimated to the crate in which he will be traveling, and give him one of his favorite toys in the crate. Do not feed the dog for several hours prior to checking in so that you minimize his need to relieve himself. Some airlines require you to provide documentation as to when the dog was last fed. In any case, a light meal is best. For long trips, you will have to attach food and water bowls to the outside of the dog's crate so that airline employees can tend to him between legs of the trip.

Make sure that your dog is properly identified and that your contact information appears on his ID tags and on his crate. Your AuCaDo will travel in a different area of the plane than the human passengers, so every rule must be strictly followed to prevent any risk of getting separated from your dog.

VACATIONS AND BOARDING

So you want to take a family vacation—and you want to include *all* members of the

COLLAR REQUIRED

If your dog gets lost, he is not able to ask for directions home. Identification tags fastened to the collar give important information—the dog's name, the owner's name, the owner's address and a telephone number where the owner can be reached. This makes it easy for whomever finds the dog to contact the owner and arrange to have the dog returned. An added advantage is that a person will be more likely to approach a lost dog who has ID tags on his collar; it tells the person that this is somebody's pet rather than a stray. This is the easiest and fastest method of identification, provided that the tags stay on the collar and the collar stays on the dog.

family. You would probably make arrangements for accommodations ahead of time anyway, but this is especially important when traveling with a dog. You do not want to make an overnight stop at the only place around for miles, only to find out that the establishment does not allow dogs. Also, you do not want to reserve a place for your family without confirming that you are traveling with a dog, because, if it is against the hotel's policy, you may end up without a place to stay.

Alternatively, if you are traveling and choose not to bring your AuCaDo, you will have to make arrangements for him while you are away. Some options are to take him to a friend's house to stay while you are gone, to have a trusted neighbor stop by often or stay at your house or to bring your dog to a reputable boarding kennel. If you choose to board him at a kennel, you should visit in advance to see the facilities provided and where the dogs are

Select a boarding kennel before you actually need one. Among your considerations should be convenience, cost, cleanliness and spaciousness. Ask for recommendations from your vet and other dog owners.

IDENTIFICATION OPTIONS

As puppies become more and more expensive, especially those puppies of high quality for showing and/or breeding, they have a greater chance of being stolen. The usual collar dog tag is, of course, easily removed. But there are two more permanent techniques that have become widely used for identification.

The puppy microchip implantation involves the injection of a small microchip, about the size of a corn kernel, under the skin of the dog. If your dog shows up at a clinic or shelter, or is offered for resale under less-than-savory circumstances, he can be positively identified by the microchip. The microchip is scanned, and a registry quickly identifies you as the owner.

Tattooing is done on various parts of the dog, from his belly to his ears. The number tattooed can be your telephone number, your dog's registration number or any other number that you can easily memorize. When professional dog thieves see a tattooed dog, they usually lose interest. For the safety of our dogs, no laboratory facility or dog broker will accept a tattooed dog as stock.

Discuss microchipping and tattooing with your veterinarian and breeder. Some vets perform these services on their own premises for a reasonable fee. To ensure that your dog's identification is effective, be certain that the dog is then properly registered with a legitimate national database.

kept. Are the dogs' areas spacious and kept clean? Talk to some of the employees and observe how they treat the dogs—do they spend time with the dogs, play with them, exercise them, etc.? Also find out the kennel's policy on vaccinations and what they require. This is for all of the dogs' safety, since there is a greater risk of diseases being passed from dog to dog when dogs are kept together.

IDENTIFICATION

Your Australian Cattle Dog is your valued companion and friend. That is why you always keep a close eye on him and you have made sure that he cannot escape from the yard or wriggle out of his collar and run away from you. However, accidents can happen and there may come a time when your dog unexpectedly becomes separated from you. If this unfortunate event should occur, the first thing on your mind will be finding him. Proper identification, including an ID tag, a tattoo and possibly a microchip, will increase the chances of his being returned to you safely and quickly.

TRAINING YOUR

AUSTRALIAN CATTLE DOG

SAFETY FIRST

While it may seem that the most important things to your dog are eating, sleeping and chewing the upholstery on your furniture, his first concern is actually safety. The domesticated dogs we keep as companions have the same pack instinct as their ancestors who ran free thousands of years ago. Because of this pack instinct, your dog wants to know that he and his pack are not in danger of being harmed, and that his pack has a strong, capable leader. You must establish yourself as the leader early on in your relationship. That way your dog will trust that you will take care of him and the pack, and he will accept your commands without question.

Living with an untrained dog is a lot like owning a piano that you do not know how to play—it is a nice object to look at, but it does not do much more than that to bring you pleasure. Now try taking piano lessons, and suddenly the piano comes alive and brings forth magical sounds and rhythms that set your heart singing and your body swaying.

The same is true with your Australian Cattle Dog. Any dog is a big responsibility and, if not trained sensibly, may develop unacceptable behavior that annoys you or could even cause family friction.

To train your Australian Cattle Dog, you may like to enroll in an obedience class. Teach your dog good manners as you learn how and why he behaves the way he does. Find out how to communicate with your dog and how to recognize and understand his communications with you. Suddenly the dog takes on a new role in your life—he is clever, interesting, well behaved and fun to be with. He demonstrates his bond of devotion to you daily. In other words, your Australian Cattle Dog does wonders for your ego because he constantly reminds you that you are not only his leader, you are his hero!

Those involved with teaching dog obedience and counseling owners about their dogs' behavior

Underneath that sweet puppy face is the strong will of an Australian Cattle Dog! It's best to teach your pup the rules early on before he starts enforcing his own laws.

FEAR AGGRESSION

Pups who are subjected to physical abuse during training commonly end up with behavioral problems as adults. One common result of abuse is fear aggression, in which a dog will lash out, bare his teeth, snarl and finally bite someone by whom he feels threatened. For example, your daughter may be playing with the dog one afternoon. As they play hide-and-seek, she backs the dog into a corner and, as she attempts to tease him playfully, he bites her hand. Examine the cause of this behavior. Did your daughter ever hit the dog? Did someone who resembles your daughter hit or scream at the dog?

Fortunately, fear aggression is relatively easy to correct. Have your daughter engage in only positive activities with the dog, such as feeding, petting and walking. She should not give any corrections or negative feedback. If the dog still growls or cowers away from her, allow someone else to accompany them. After approximately one week, the dog should feel that he can rely on her for many positive things, and he will also be prevented from reacting fearfully towards anyone who might resemble her.

have discovered some interesting facts about dog ownership. For example, training dogs when they are puppies results in the highest rate of success in developing well-mannered and well-adjusted adult dogs. Training an older dog, from six months to six years of age, can produce almost equal results, providing that the owner accepts the dog's slower rate of learning capability and is willing to work patiently to help the dog succeed at developing to his fullest potential. Unfortunately, many owners of untrained adult dogs lack the patience factor, so they do not persist until their dogs are successful at learning particular behaviors.

Training a puppy aged 10 to 16 weeks (20 weeks at the most) is like working with a dry sponge in a pool of water. The pup soaks up whatever you show him and constantly looks for more things to do and learn. At this early age, his body is not yet producing hormones, and therein lies the reason for such a high rate of success. Without hormones, he is focused on his owner and not particularly interested in investi-

gating other places, dogs, people, etc. You are his leader: his provider of food, water, shelter and security. He latches onto you and wants to stay close. He will usually follow you from room to room, will not let you out of his sight when you are outdoors with him and will respond in like manner to the people and animals you encounter. If you greet a friend warmly, he will be happy to greet the person as well. If, however, you are hesitant or anxious about the approach of a stranger, he will respond accordingly.

Once the puppy begins to produce hormones, his natural curiosity emerges and he begins to investigate the world around him. It is at this time when you may notice that the untrained dog begins to wander away from you and even ignore your commands to stay close. When this behavior becomes a problem, you have two choices: get rid of the dog or train him. It is strongly urged that you choose the latter option.

You usually will be able to find obedience classes within a reasonable distance from your home, but you can also do a lot to train your dog yourself. Sometimes there are classes available, but the tuition is too costly. Whatever the circumstances, the solution to training your dog without formal obedience classes lies within the

> ### REAP THE REWARDS
> If you start with a normal, healthy dog and give him time, patience and some carefully executed lessons, you will reap the rewards of that training for the life of the dog. And what a life it will be! The two of you will find immeasurable pleasure in the companionship you have built together with love, respect and understanding.

pages of this book. This chapter is devoted to helping you train your Australian Cattle Dog at home. If the recommended procedures are followed faithfully, you may expect positive results that will prove rewarding both to you and your dog.

Whether your new charge is a puppy or a mature adult, the methods of teaching and the techniques we use in training basic behaviors are the same. After all, no dog, whether puppy or adult, likes harsh or inhumane treatment. All creatures, however, respond favorably to gentle motivational methods and sincere praise and encouragement. Now let us get started.

HOUSE-TRAINING
You can train a puppy to relieve himself wherever you choose, but this must be somewhere suitable. You should bear in mind from the outset that when your puppy is old enough to go out in public places, any canine droppings must be removed at once. You will always have to carry with you a small plastic bag or "poop-scoop."

Outdoor training includes such surfaces as grass, soil and cement. Indoor training usually means training your dog to newspaper. When deciding on the surface and location that you will want your Australian Cattle Dog to use, be sure it is going to be permanent. Training your dog to grass and then changing your mind a few months later is extremely difficult for both dog and owner.

Next, choose the command you will use each and every time you want your puppy to void. "Hurry up" and "Let's go" are examples of commands commonly used by dog owners. Get in the habit of giving the puppy your chosen relief command before you take him out. That way, when he becomes an adult, you will be able to determine if he wants to go out

House-training is the key to clean and harmonious living with a dog of any breed.

when you ask him. A confirmation will be signs of interest, such as wagging his tail, watching you intently, going to the door, etc.

PUPPY'S NEEDS

Your new puppy needs to relieve himself after play periods, after each meal, after he has been sleeping and at any time he indicates that he is looking for a place to urinate or defecate. The urinary and intestinal tract

---

TAKE THE LEAD

Do not carry your dog to his relief area. Lead him there on a leash or, better yet, encourage him to follow you to the spot. If you start carrying him to his spot, you might end up doing this routine forever and your dog will have the satisfaction of having trained *you*.

muscles of very young puppies are not fully developed. Therefore, like human babies, puppies need to relieve themselves frequently.

Take your puppy out often—every hour for an eight-week-old, for example—and always immediately after sleeping and eating. The older the puppy, the less often he will need to relieve himself. Finally, as a mature healthy adult, he will require only three to five relief trips per day.

HOUSING

Since the types of housing and control you provide for your puppy have a direct relationship on the success of house-training, we consider the various aspects of both before we begin training.

Taking a new puppy home and turning him loose in your house can be compared to turning a child loose in an amusement park and telling the child that the place is all his! The sheer enormity of the place would be too much for him to handle. Instead, offer the puppy clearly defined areas where he can play, sleep, eat and live. A room of the house where the family gathers is the most obvious choice. Puppies are social animals and need to feel a part of the pack right from the start. Hearing your voice, watching you while you are doing things and smelling you nearby are all positive reinforcers that he

CANINE DEVELOPMENT SCHEDULE

It is important to understand how and at what age a puppy develops into adulthood.
If you are a puppy owner, consult the following Canine Development Schedule to
determine the stage of development your puppy is currently experiencing.
This knowledge will help you as you work with the puppy in the weeks and months ahead.

Period	Age	Characteristics
FIRST TO THIRD	BIRTH TO SEVEN WEEKS	Puppy needs food, sleep and warmth, and responds to simple and gentle touching. Needs mother for security and disciplining. Needs littermates for learning and interacting with other dogs. Pup learns to function within a pack and learns pack order of dominance. Begin socializing pup with adults and children for short periods. Pup begins to become aware of his environment.
FOURTH	EIGHT TO TWELVE WEEKS	Brain is fully developed. Pup needs socializing with outside world. Remove from mother and littermates. Needs to change from canine pack to human pack. Human dominance necessary. Fear period occurs between 8 and 12 weeks. Avoid fright and pain.
FIFTH	THIRTEEN TO SIXTEEN WEEKS	Training and formal obedience should begin. Less association with other dogs, more with people, places, situations. Period will pass easily if you remember this is pup's change-to-adolescence time. Be firm and fair. Flight instinct prominent. Permissiveness and over-disciplining can do permanent damage. Praise for good behavior.
JUVENILE	FOUR TO EIGHT MONTHS	Another fear period about 7 to 8 months of age. It passes quickly, but be cautious of fright and pain. Sexual maturity reached. Dominant traits established. Dog should understand sit, down, come and stay by now.

NOTE: THESE ARE APPROXIMATE TIME FRAMES. ALLOW FOR INDIVIDUAL DIFFERENCES IN PUPPIES.

is now a member of your pack. Usually a family room, the kitchen or a nearby adjoining breakfast area is ideal for providing safety and security for both puppy and owner.

Within the designated room, there should be a smaller area that the puppy can call his own. An alcove, a wire or fiberglass dog crate or a partitioned-off (not boarded!) corner from which he can view the activities of his new family will be fine. The size of the area or crate is the key factor here. The area must be large enough so that the puppy can lie down and stretch out, as well as stand up,

THE SUCCESS METHOD

Success that comes by luck is usually short-lived. Success that comes by well-thought-out proven methods is often more easily achieved and permanent. This is the Success Method. It is designed to give you, the puppy owner, a simple yet proven way to help your puppy develop clean living habits and a feeling of security in his new environment.

6 Steps to Successful Crate Training

1 Tell the puppy "Crate time!" and place him in the crate with a small treat (a piece of cheese or half of a biscuit). Let him stay in the crate for five minutes while you are in the same room. Then release him and praise lavishly. Never release him when he is fussing. Wait until he is quiet before you let him out.

2 Repeat Step 1 several times a day.

3 The next day, place the puppy in the crate as before. Let him stay there for ten minutes. Do this several times.

4 Continue building time in five-minute increments until the puppy stays in his crate for 30 minutes with you in the room. Always take him to his relief area after prolonged periods in his crate.

5 Now go back to Step 1 and let the puppy stay in his crate for five minutes, this time while you are out of the room.

6 Once again, build crate time in five-minute increments with you out of the room. When the puppy will stay willingly in his crate (he may even fall asleep!) for 30 minutes with you out of the room, he will be ready to stay in it for several hours at a time.

without rubbing his head on the top. At the same time, it must be small enough so that he cannot relieve himself at one end and sleep at the other without coming into contact with his droppings. Dogs are, by nature, clean animals and will not remain close to their relief areas unless forced to do so. In those cases, they then become dirty dogs and usually remain that way for life.

The dog's designated area should contain clean bedding and a toy. Once house-training is accomplished, water must always be available, in a non-spill container.

CONTROL

By *control*, we mean helping the puppy to create a lifestyle pattern that will be compatible to that of his human pack (you!). Just as we guide little children to learn our way of life, we must show the puppy when it is time to play, eat, sleep, exercise and even entertain himself.

Your puppy should always sleep in his crate. He should also learn that, during times of household confusion and excessive human activity, such as at breakfast when family members are preparing for the day, he can play by himself in relative safety and comfort in his designated area. Each time you leave the puppy alone, he should under-stand exactly where he is to stay.

FAMILY TIES
If you have other pets in the home and/or interact often with the pets of friends and other family members, your pup will respond to those pets in much the same manner as you do. It is only when you show fear of or resent-ment toward another animal that he will act fearful or unfriendly.

Puppies are chewers and cannot tell the difference between things like lamp cords, television wires, shoes, table legs, etc. Chewing into a television wire, for example, can be fatal to the puppy, while a shorted wire can start a fire in the house. If the puppy chews on the arm of the chair when he is alone, you will probably discipline him angrily when you get home. Thus, he makes the association that your coming home means he is going to be punished. (He will not remember chewing the chair and is incapable of making the association of the discipline with his naughty deed.) Accustoming the pup to his designated area not only keeps him safe but also avoids his engaging in destructive behaviors when you are not there to supervise.

Times of excitement, such as special occasions, family parties, etc., can be fun for the puppy, providing that he can view the activities from the security of his designated area. He is not underfoot and he is not being fed all sorts of tidbits that will probably cause him stomach distress, yet he still feels a part of the fun.

ESTABLISHING A SCHEDULE

A puppy should be taken to his relief area each time he is released

Whether it's his crate, bed or other area of his own, indoors or out, house-training is based on the fact that a dog does not like to soil areas in which he spends time.

from his designated area, after meals, after play sessions and when he first awakens in the morning (at age eight weeks, this can mean 5 a.m.!). The puppy will indicate that he's ready "to go" by circling or sniffing busily—do not misinterpret these signs. For a puppy less than ten weeks of age, a routine of taking him out every hour is necessary. As the puppy grows, he will be able to wait for longer periods of time.

Keep trips to his relief area short. Stay no more than five or six minutes and then return to the house. If he goes during that time, praise him lavishly and take him indoors immediately. If he does not, but he has an accident when you go

back indoors, pick him up immediately, say "No! No!" and return to his relief area. Wait a few minutes, then return to the house again. Never hit a puppy or put his face in urine or excrement when he has had an accident!

Once indoors, put the puppy in his crate until you have had time to clean up his accident. Then, release him to the family area and watch him more closely than before. Chances are, his accident was a result of your not picking up his signal or waiting too long before offering him the opportunity to relieve himself. Never hold a grudge against the puppy for accidents.

Let the puppy learn that going outdoors means it is time to relieve himself, not to play. Once trained, he will be able to play indoors and out and still differentiate between the times for play versus the times for relief. Help him develop regular hours for naps, being alone, playing by himself and just resting, all in his crate. Encourage him to entertain himself while you are busy with your activities. Let him learn that having you near is comforting, but it is not your main purpose in life to provide him with undivided attention. Each time you put your puppy in his own area, use the same command, whatever suits best. Soon he will run to his crate or special area when he hears you say those words.

HOW MANY TIMES A DAY?

AGE	RELIEF TRIPS
To 14 weeks	10
14–22 weeks	8
22–32 weeks	6
Adulthood (dog stops growing)	4

These are estimates, of course, but they are a guide to the *minimum* number of opportunities a dog should have each day to relieve himself.

Crate training provides safety for you, the puppy and the home. It also provides the puppy with a feeling of security, and that helps the puppy achieve self-confidence and clean habits. Remember that one of the primary ingredients in house-training your puppy is control. Regardless of your lifestyle, there will always be occasions when you will need to have a place where your dog can stay and be happy and safe. Crate

TRAINING RULES

If you want to be successful in training your dog, you have four rules to obey yourself:
1. Develop an understanding of how a dog thinks.
2. Do not blame the dog for lack of communication.
3. Define your dog's personality and act accordingly.
4. Have patience and be consistent.

training is the answer for now and in the future.

In conclusion, a few key elements are really all you need for a successful house-training method—consistency, frequency, praise, control and supervision. By following these procedures with a normal, healthy puppy, you and the puppy will soon be past the stage of "accidents" and ready to move on to a clean and rewarding life together.

ROLES OF DISCIPLINE, REWARD AND PUNISHMENT

Discipline, training one to act in accordance with rules, brings order to life. It is as simple as that. Without discipline, particularly in a group society, chaos will reign supreme and the group will eventually perish. Humans and canines are social animals and need some form of discipline in order to function effectively. They must procure food, reproduce to keep their species going and protect their home base and their young. If there were no discipline in the lives of social animals, they would eventually die from starvation and/or predation by other stronger animals. In the case of domestic canines, discipline in their lives is needed in order for them to understand how their pack (you and other family members) functions and how they must act in order to survive.

A large humane society in a highly populated area recently surveyed dog owners regarding their satisfaction with their relationships with their dogs. People who had trained their dogs were 75% more satisfied with their pets than those who had never trained their dogs.

Dr. Edward Thorndike, a noted psychologist, established *Thorndike's Theory of Learning*, which states that a behavior that results in a pleasant event tends to be repeated. Furthermore, it concludes that a behavior that results in an unpleasant event tends not to be repeated. It is this theory upon which training methods are based today. For example, if you manipulate a dog to perform a specific behavior and reward him for doing it, he is likely to do it again because he enjoyed the end result.

Occasionally, punishment, a penalty inflicted for an offense, is necessary. The best type of punishment often comes from an outside source. For example, a child is told not to touch the stove because he may get burned. He disobeys and touches the stove. In doing so, he receives a burn. From that time on, he respects the heat of the stove and avoids contact with it. Therefore, a behavior that results in an unpleasant event tends not to be repeated.

A good example of a dog's learning the hard way is the dog who chases the house cat. He is told many times to leave the cat alone, yet he persists in teasing

THINK BEFORE YOU BARK
Dogs are sensitive to their masters' moods and emotions. Use your voice wisely when communicating with your dog. Never raise your voice at your dog unless you are trying to correct him. "Barking" at your dog can become as meaningless as "dogspeak" is to you.

the cat. Then, one day, the dog begins chasing the cat but the cat turns and swipes a claw across the dog's face, leaving the dog with a painful gash on his nose. The final result is that the dog stops chasing the cat.

TRAINING EQUIPMENT

COLLAR AND LEAD
For an Australian Cattle Dog, the collar and lead that you use for training must be one with which

you are easily able to work, not too heavy for the dog and perfectly safe.

TREATS

Have a bag of treats on hand; something nutritious and easy to swallow works best. Use a soft treat, a chunk of cheese or a piece of cooked chicken rather than a dry biscuit. By the time the dog has finished chewing a dry treat, he will forget why he is being rewarded in the first place!

In training, rewarding the dog with a food treat will help him associate praise and the treats with learning new behaviors that obviously please

---

CALM DOWN
Dogs will do anything for your attention. If you reward the dog when he is calm and attentive, you will develop a well-mannered dog. If, on the other hand, you greet your dog excitedly and encourage him to wrestle with you, the dog will greet you the same way and you will have a hyperactive dog on your hands.

---

his owner. Using food rewards will not teach a dog to beg at the table—the only way to teach a dog to beg at the table is to give him food from the table.

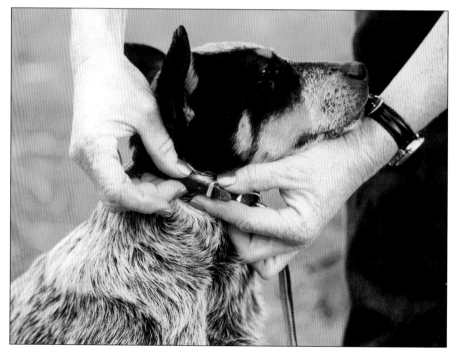

Choose a lightweight yet sturdy buckle collar that can be adjusted to fit your AuCaDo safely and comfortably.

TRAINING BEGINS: ASK THE DOG A QUESTION

In order to teach your dog anything, you must first get his attention. After all, he cannot learn anything if he is looking away from you with his mind on something else.

To get your dog's attention, ask him "School?" and immediately walk over to him and give him a treat as you tell him "Good dog." Wait a minute or two and repeat the routine, this time with a treat in your hand as you approach within a foot of the dog. Do not go directly to him, but stop about a foot short of him and hold out the treat as you ask "School?" He will see you approaching with a treat in your hand and most likely begin walking toward you. As you meet, give him the treat and praise again.

The third time, ask the question, have a treat in your hand and walk only a short

The next step is attaching the lead, making sure that the clasp closes securely.

distance toward the dog so that he must walk almost all the way to you. As he reaches you, give him the treat and praise again.

By this time, the dog will probably be getting the idea that if he pays attention to you, especially when you ask that question, it will pay off in treats and enjoyable activities for him. In other words, he learns that "school" means doing great things with you that are fun and that result in positive attention for him.

Remember that the dog does not understand your verbal language; he only recognizes sounds. Your question translates to a series of sounds for him, and those sounds become the signal to go to you and pay attention. The dog learns that if he does this, he will get to interact with you plus receive treats and praise.

THE GOLDEN RULE

The golden rule of dog training is simple. For each "question" (command), there is only one correct answer (reaction). One command = one reaction. Keep practicing the command until the dog reacts correctly without hesitating. Be repetitive but not monotonous and keep training sessions short. Dogs get bored just as people do!

READY, SIT, GO!

On your marks, get set: train! Most professional trainers agree that the sit command is the place to start your dog's formal education. Sitting is a natural posture for most dogs and they respond to the sit exercise willingly and readily. For every lesson, begin with the sit command, so that you start out on a successful note. Likewise, you should practice the sit command at the end of every lesson as well because you always want to end on a high note.

THE BASIC COMMANDS FOR OBEDIENCE TRAINING

TEACHING SIT

Now that you have the dog's attention, attach his lead and hold it in your left hand, and hold a food treat in your right hand. Place your food hand at the dog's nose and let him lick the treat but not take it from you. Say "Sit" and slowly raise your food hand from in front of the dog's nose up over his head so that he is looking at the ceiling. As he bends his head upward, he will have to bend his knees to maintain his balance. As he bends his knees, he will assume a sit position. At that point, release the food treat and praise lavishly with comments such as "Good dog! Good sit!," etc. Remember to always praise enthusiastically, because dogs relish verbal praise from their owners and feel so proud of themselves whenever they accomplish a behavior.

You will not use food forever in getting the dog to obey your commands. Food is only used to teach new behaviors and, once the dog knows what you want when you give a specific command, you will wean him off the food treats but still maintain the verbal praise. After all, you will always have your voice with you, and there will be many times when you have no food rewards but expect the dog to obey.

TEACHING DOWN

Teaching the down exercise is easy when you understand how the dog perceives the down position, and it is very difficult when you do not. Dogs perceive the down position as a submissive one; therefore, teaching the down exercise by using a forceful method can sometimes make the dog develop such a fear of the down that he either runs away when you say "Down" or he attempts to snap at the person who tries to force him down.

Have the dog sit close alongside your left leg, facing in the same direction as you are. Hold the lead in your left hand and a food treat in your right. Now place your left hand lightly on the top of the dog's shoulders where they meet above the spinal cord. Do not push down on the dog's shoulders; simply rest your left hand there so you can guide the dog to lie down close to your left leg rather than to swing away from your side when he drops.

Now place the food hand at the dog's nose, say "Down" very softly (almost a whisper) and slowly lower the food hand to the dog's front feet. When the food hand reaches the floor, begin moving it forward along the floor in front of the dog. Keep talking softly to the dog, saying things like, "Do you want this treat? You can do this, good dog." Your reassuring tone of voice will help calm the dog as he tries to follow the food hand in order to get the treat.

When the dog's elbows touch the floor, release the food and praise softly. Try to get the dog to maintain that down position for several seconds before you let him sit up again. The goal here is to get the dog to settle down and not feel threatened in the down position.

Attention is the key to success in the show ring and, in fact, to any training endeavor with your Australian Cattle Dog.

CONSISTENCY PAYS OFF

Dogs need consistency in their feeding schedule, exercise and relief visits, and in the verbal commands you use. If you use "Stay" on Monday and "Stay here, please" on Tuesday, you will confuse your dog. Don't demand perfect behavior during training sessions and then let him have the run of the house the rest of the day. Above all, lavish praise on your pet consistently every time he does something right. The more he feels he is pleasing you, the more willing he will be to learn.

TEACHING STAY

It is easy to teach the dog to stay in either a sit or a down position. Again, we use food and praise during the teaching process as we help the dog to understand exactly what it is that we are expecting him to do.

To teach the sit/stay, start with the dog sitting on your left side as before and hold the lead in your left hand. Have a food treat in your right hand and place your food hand at the dog's nose. Say "Stay" and step out on your right foot to stand directly in front of the dog, toe to toe, as he licks and nibbles the treat. Be sure to keep his head facing upward to maintain the sit position. Count to five and then swing around to stand next to the dog again with him on your left. As soon as you get back to the original position, release the food and praise lavishly.

To teach the down/stay, do the down as previously described. As soon as the dog lies down, say "Stay" and step out on your right foot just as you did in the sit/stay. Count to five and then return to stand beside the dog with him on your left side. Release the treat and praise as always.

Within a week or ten days, you can begin to add a bit of distance between you and your dog when you leave him. When you do, use your left hand open with the palm facing the dog as a stay signal, much the same as the hand signal a police officer uses to stop traffic at an intersection. Hold the food treat in your right hand as before, but this time the food will not be touching the dog's nose. He will watch the food hand and quickly learn that he is going to get that treat as soon as you return to his side.

When you can stand 3 feet away from your dog for 30 seconds, you can then begin building time and distance in both stays. Eventually, the dog can be expected to remain in the stay position for prolonged periods of time until you return to him or call him to you. Always praise lavishly when he stays.

TEACHING COME

If you make teaching "come" an exciting experience, you should never have a student that does not love the game or that fails to come when called. The secret, it seems, is never to teach the word "come."

At times when an owner most wants his dog to come when called, the owner is likely to be upset or anxious and he allows these feelings to come through in the tone of his voice when he calls his dog. Hearing that desperation in his owner's voice, the dog fears the results of going to him and therefore either disobeys outright or runs in the opposite direction. The secret, therefore, is

to teach the dog a game and, when you want him to come to you, simply play the game. It is practically a no-fail solution!

To begin, have several members of your family take a few food treats and each go into a different room in the house. Everyone takes turns calling the dog, and each person should celebrate the dog's finding him with a treat and lots of happy praise. When a person calls the dog, he is actually inviting the dog to find him and to get a treat as a reward for "winning."

A few turns of the "Where are you?" game and the dog will

> ### "COME" . . . BACK
> Never call your dog to come to you for a correction or scold him when he reaches you. That is the quickest way to turn a come command into "Go away fast!" Dogs think only in the present tense, and your dog will connect the scolding with coming to you, not with the misbehavior of a few moments earlier.

understand that everyone is playing the game and that each person has a big celebration awaiting the dog's success at locating him or her. Once the dog learns to love the game, simply calling out "Where are you?" will bring him running from wherever he is when he hears that all-important question.

The come command is recognized as one of the most important things to teach a dog, but there are trainers who work with thousands of dogs and never use the actual word "come." Yet these dogs will race to respond to a person who uses the dog's name followed by "Where are you?" For example, a woman has a 12-year-old companion dog who went blind, but who never fails to locate her owner when asked, "Where are you?"

Children, in particular, love to play this game with their dogs. Children can hide in smaller places like a shower stall or bathtub, behind a bed or under a table. The dog needs to work a little bit harder to find these hiding places, but, when he does, he loves to celebrate with a treat and a tussle with a favorite youngster.

TEACHING HEEL

It's time to teach the Heeler to heel! Not referring to nipping cattle, heeling means that the dog walks beside the owner without pulling. It takes time and patience on the owner's part to succeed at teaching the dog that he (the owner) will not proceed unless the dog is walking calmly beside him. Neither pulling out ahead on the lead nor lagging behind is acceptable.

Begin by holding the lead in your left hand as the dog sits beside your left leg. Move the loop end of the lead to your right hand, but keep your left hand short on the lead so that it keeps the dog in close next to you.

Say "Heel" and step forward

THE STUDENT'S STRESS TEST

During training sessions, you must be able to recognize signs of stress in your dog such as:

- tucking his tail between his legs
- lowering his head
- shivering or trembling
- standing completely still or running away
- panting and/or salivating
- avoiding eye contact
- flattening his ears back
- urinating submissively
- rolling over and lifting a leg
- grinning or baring teeth
- aggression when restrained

If your four-legged student displays these signs, he may just be nervous or intimidated. The training session may have been too lengthy, with not enough praise and affirmation. Stop for the day and try again tomorrow.

on your left foot. Keep the dog close to you and take three steps. Stop and have the dog sit next to you in what we now call the heel position. Praise verbally, but do not touch the dog. Hesitate a moment and begin again with "Heel," taking three steps and stopping, at which point the dog is told to sit again.

Your goal here is to have the dog walk those three steps without pulling on the lead. Once he will walk calmly beside you for three steps without pulling, increase the number of steps you take to five. When he will walk politely beside you while you take five steps, you can increase the length of your walk to ten steps. Keep increasing the length of your stroll until the dog will walk quietly beside you without pulling as long as you want him to heel. When you stop heeling, indicate to the dog that the exercise is over by verbally praising as you pet him and say, "OK, good dog." The "OK" is used as a release word, meaning that

Show dogs demonstrate their knowledge of the heel command as they gait in the show ring. Heeling, however, is necessary for *all* dogs, not just show dogs.

the exercise is finished and the dog is free to relax.

If you are dealing with a dog who insists on pulling you around, simply "put on your brakes" and stand your ground until the dog realizes that the two of you are not going anywhere until he is beside you and moving at your pace, not his. It may take some time just standing there to convince the dog that you are the leader and that you will be the one to decide on the direction and speed of your travel.

Each time the dog looks up at you or slows down to give a slack lead between the two of you, quietly praise him and say, "Good heel. Good dog." Eventually, the dog will begin to respond and within a few days he will be walking politely beside you without pulling on the lead. At first, the training sessions should

TUG OF WALK?

If you begin teaching the heel by taking long walks and letting the dog pull you along, he misinterprets this action as an acceptable form of taking a walk. When you pull back on the leash to counteract his pulling, he reads that tug as a signal to pull even harder!

Your puppy should be taught to obey commands from all members of the family. Once trained to heel, he should behave so politely on lead that even a child can walk him.

WEANING OFF FOOD IN TRAINING

Food is used in training new behaviors. Once the dog understands what behavior goes with a specific command, it is time to start weaning him off the food treats. At first, give a treat after each exercise. Then, start to give a treat only after every other exercise. Mix up the times when you offer a food reward and the times when you only offer praise so that the dog will never know when he is going to receive both food and praise and when he is going to receive only praise. This is called a variable-ratio reward system. It proves successful because there is always the chance that the owner will produce a treat, so the dog never stops trying for that reward. No matter what, *always* give verbal praise.

be kept short and very positive; soon the dog will be able to walk nicely with you for increasingly longer distances. Remember also to give the dog free time and the opportunity to run and play when you have finished heel practice.

HEELING WELL

Teach your dog to heel in an enclosed area. Once you think the dog will obey reliably and you want to attempt advanced obedience exercises such as off-lead heeling, test him in a fenced-in area so he cannot run away.

OBEDIENCE CLASSES

It is a good idea to enroll in an obedience class if one is available in your area. If yours is a show dog, classes to prepare for the show ring would be more appropriate. Many areas have dog clubs that offer basic obedience training as well as preparatory classes for obedience competition. There are also local dog trainers who offer similar classes.

At obedience trials, dogs can earn titles at various levels of

PLAN TO PLAY
The puppy should also have regular play and exercise sessions when he is with you or a family member. Exercise for a very young puppy can consist of a short walk around the house or yard. Playing can include fetching games with a large ball or a special toy. (All puppies teethe and need soft things upon which to chew.) Remember to restrict play periods to indoors within his living area (the family room, for example) until he is completely house-trained.

competition. The beginning levels of obedience competition include basic behaviors such as sit, down, heel, etc. The more advanced levels of competition include jumping, retrieving, scent discrimination and signal work. The advanced levels require a dog and owner to put a lot of time and effort into their training. The titles that can be earned at these levels of competition are very prestigious.

OTHER ACTIVITIES FOR LIFE
Whether a dog is trained in the structured environment of a class or alone with his owner at home, there are many activities that can bring fun and rewards to both owner and dog once they have mastered basic control.

Teaching the dog to help out around the home, in the yard or on the farm provides great satisfaction to both dog and owner. In addition, the dog's help makes life a little easier for his owner and raises his stature as a valued companion to his family. It helps give the dog a purpose by occupying his mind and providing an outlet for his energy.

Backpacking is an exciting and healthy activity that the dog can be taught without assistance from more than his owner. The exercise of walking and climbing is good for man and dog alike, and the bond that they develop together is priceless. The rule for backpacking with any dog is never to expect the dog to carry more than one-sixth of his body weight.

More dogs mean more training. It would be quite a task to handle multiple Australian Cattle Dogs if each were not trained reliably to the basic commands.

HELPING PAWS
Your dog may not be the next Lassie, but every pet has the potential to do some tricks well. Identify his natural talents and hone them. Is your dog always happy and upbeat? Teach him to wag his tail or give you his paw on command. Real homebodies can be trained to do household chores, such as carrying dirty laundry or retrieving the morning paper.

If you are interested in participating in organized competition with your Australian Cattle Dog, there are activities other than obedience in which you and your dog can become involved. Herding tests and trials are held by the AKC and breed clubs, as well as by specialty clubs that cater to herding breeds. Whether or not your AuCaDo is a working dog, he will revel in the opportunity to put his instincts to use and to show off his innate skills, doing what he was bred to do in a competitive setting.

Another competitive canine venue is agility. Agility is a popular sport in which dogs run through obstacle courses that include various jumps, tunnels and other exercises to test the dog's speed and coordination. The owners run beside their dogs to give commands and to guide them through the course. Although competitive, the focus is on fun—it's fun to do, fun to watch and great exercise for dog and handler alike.

The range of activities you can do with your AuCaDo are practically endless. In addition to those mentioned, your dog will enjoy hiking, cart pulling, square dancing and trick training. You name it! Keeping in mind how athletic your dog is, you will find any of these activities fun and rewarding for both you and your dog. Check with the AKC, the national breed club and local dog clubs to learn about what sports are available to dogs and owners in your area. Not only will clubs know of dog-related activities in your locality but they also will be able to give you the contact information of other owners who participate in these activities with their dogs.

Finally, be sure to talk to your dog's breeder about the availability of activities for your dog. You will probably be invited to join other AuCaDo owners with similar interests in doing things with their dogs. Be sure to take advantage of every opportunity to meet other dog people and learn about what they are doing with their canine companions. Sooner or later, you'll find the perfect lifestyle for you and your own Australian Cattle Dog. Whatever you choose, get out there and enjoy life with your Australian Cattle Dog!

KEEP SMILING

Never train your dog, puppy or adult, when you are angry or in a sour mood. Dogs are very sensitive to human feelings, especially anger, and if your dog senses that you are angry or upset, he will connect your anger with his training and learn to resent or fear his training sessions.

Home on the range! An AuCaDo will thrive in a farm environment, where he will be in his element and never lacking for things to do.

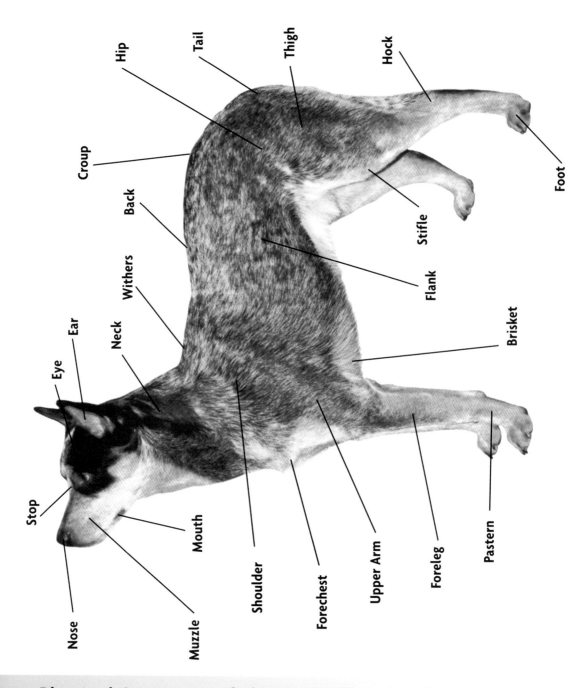

Tail

Hip

Thigh

Croup

Hock

Back

Foot

Withers

Stifle

Neck

Flank

Ear

Brisket

Eye

Stop

Nose

Mouth

Muzzle

Shoulder

Forechest

Upper Arm

Foreleg

Pastern

Physical Structure of the Australian Cattle Dog

AUSTRALIAN CATTLE DOG

Dogs suffer from many of the same physical illnesses as people and might even share many of the same psychological problems. Since people usually know more about human diseases than canine maladies, many of the terms used in this chapter will be familiar but not necessarily those used by veterinarians. For example, we will use the familiar term *x-ray* instead of *radiograph*. We will also use the familiar term *symptoms*, even though dogs don't have symptoms, which are verbal descriptions of something the patient feels or observes himself that he regards as abnormal. Dogs have *clinical signs* since they cannot speak, so we have to look for these clinical signs...but we still use the term *symptoms* in this book.

Medicine is a constantly changing art, of course with scientific input as well. Things alter as we learn more and more about basic sciences such as genetics and biochemistry, and have use of more sophisticated imaging techniques like Computer Aided Tomography (CAT scans) and Magnetic Resonance Imaging

(MRI scans). There is academic dispute about many canine maladies, so different veterinarians treat them in different ways. For example, some vets place a greater emphasis on surgical treatments than others.

SELECTING A VETERINARIAN
Your selection of a veterinarian should be based on personal recommendation for his skills with small animals, especially dogs, and, if possible, especially Australian Cattle Dogs. If the vet is based nearby, it will be helpful because you might have an emergency or need to make multiple visits for treatments.

All veterinarians are licensed and should be capable of dealing with everyday medical issues such as infections, injuries, routine surgeries (spaying/ neutering, stitching up wounds, etc.) and the promotion of health (for example, by vaccination). If the problem affecting your dog is more complex, your vet will refer your pet to someone with a more detailed knowledge of what is wrong. This will usually be a specialist, perhaps at the nearest

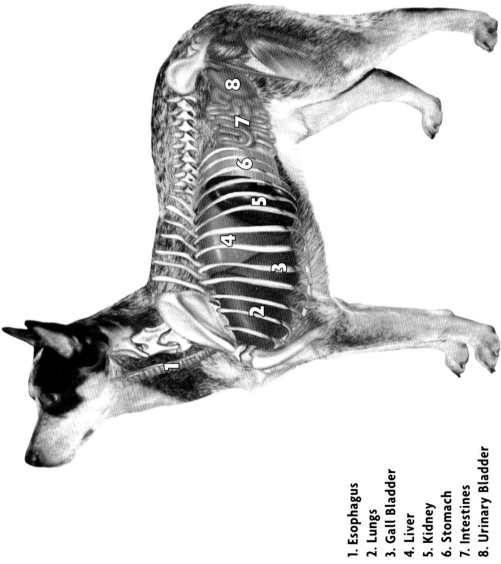

1. Esophagus
2. Lungs
3. Gall Bladder
4. Liver
5. Kidney
6. Stomach
7. Intestines
8. Urinary Bladder

Internal Organs of the Australian Cattle Dog

university veterinary school, who concentrates in the field relevant to your dog's problem.

Veterinary procedures are very costly and, as the treatments available improve, they are going to become more expensive. It is quite acceptable to discuss matters of cost with your vet; if there is more than one treatment option, cost may be a factor in deciding which route to take.

Insurance against veterinary cost is also becoming very popular. As veterinary insurance is becoming more common, a wider range of options is becoming available. Basic coverage may include emergencies only, where a more extensive policy may cover aspects of the dog's routine care, such as annual check-ups, vaccinations and parasite control.

PREVENTATIVE MEDICINE

It is much easier, less costly and more effective to practice preventative medicine than to fight bouts of illness and disease. Properly bred puppies of all breeds come from parents that were selected based upon their genetic-disease profiles. The puppies' mother should have been vaccinated, free of all internal and external parasites and properly nourished. For these reasons, a visit to the vet who cared for the dam is recommended if at all possible. The dam passes disease resistance

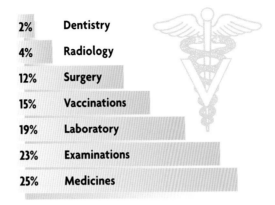

Breakdown of Veterinary Income by Category

2%	Dentistry
4%	Radiology
12%	Surgery
15%	Vaccinations
19%	Laboratory
23%	Examinations
25%	Medicines

A typical vet's income, categorized according to services performed. This survey dealt with small-animal (pets) practices.

to her puppies, which should last from eight to ten weeks. Unfortunately, she can also pass on parasites and infection. This is why knowledge about her health is useful in learning more about the health of the puppies.

WEANING TO BRINGING PUPPY HOME
Puppies should be weaned by the time they are two months old. A puppy that remains for at least eight weeks with his mother and littermates usually adapts better to other dogs and people later in life.

Sometimes new owners have their puppy examined by a veterinarian immediately, which is a good idea unless the puppy is overtired by a long journey home from the breeder's. In that case, an appointment should be arranged for the next day or two.

The puppy will have his teeth examined and his skeletal confor-

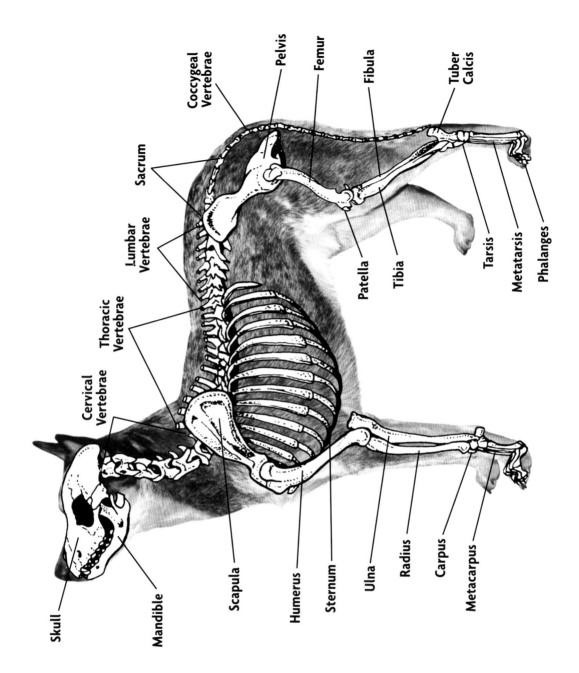

Skeletal Structure of the Australian Cattle Dog

mation and general health checked prior to certification by the veterinarian. Puppies in certain breeds have problems with their kneecaps, cataracts and other eye problems, heart murmurs and undescended testicles. Your veterinarian might also have training in temperament evaluation. At the first visit, your vet will set up a schedule for continuing your pup's vaccination program.

VACCINATIONS
Most vaccinations are given by injection and should only be given by a veterinarian. Both he and you should keep a record of the date of the injection, the identification of the vaccine and the amount given. Some vets give a first vaccination at six weeks, but most dog breeders prefer the course not to commence until about eight weeks because of the risk of interaction with the antibodies produced by the mother. The vaccination timetable is usually based on a two- to four-week cycle. You must take your vet's advice as to when to vaccinate, as this may differ according to the vaccine used.

The usual vaccines contain immunizing doses of several

HEALTH AND VACCINATION SCHEDULE

AGE IN WEEKS:	6TH	8TH	10TH	12TH	14TH	16TH	20-24TH	52ND
Worm Control	✔	✔	✔	✔	✔	✔	✔	
Neutering							✔	
Heartworm		✔		✔		✔	✔	
Parvovirus	✔		✔		✔		✔	✔
Distemper		✔		✔		✔		✔
Hepatitis		✔		✔		✔		✔
Leptospirosis								✔
Parainfluenza	✔		✔		✔			✔
Dental Examination		✔					✔	✔
Complete Physical		✔					✔	✔
Coronavirus					✔		✔	✔
Canine Cough	✔							
Hip Dysplasia							✔	
Rabies							✔	

Vaccinations are not instantly effective. It takes about two weeks for the dog's immune system to develop antibodies. Most vaccinations require annual booster shots. Your vet should guide you in this regard.

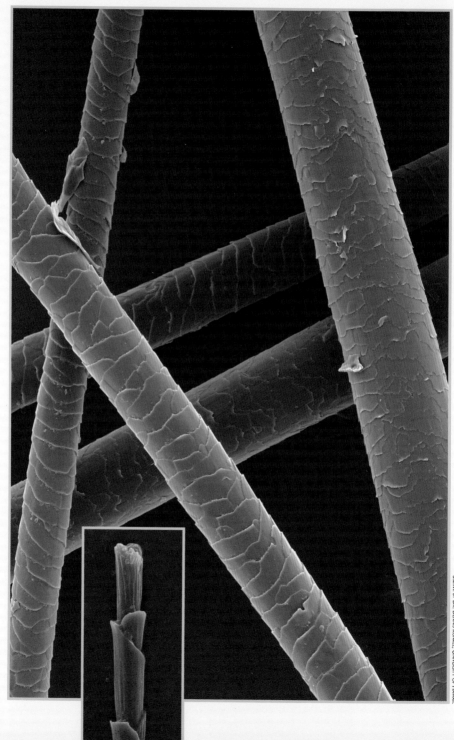

The normal, healthy hairs of a typical dog, enlarged about 200 times normal size. The inset shows the tip of a fine, growing hair about 2,000 times normal size.

different viruses such as distemper, parvovirus, parainfluenza and hepatitis. There are other vaccines available when the puppy is at risk. You should rely upon professional advice. This is especially true for the booster immunizations. Most vaccination programs require a booster when the puppy is a year old and once a year thereafter. In some cases, circumstances may require more or less frequent immunizations.

Canine cough, more formally known as tracheobronchitis, is immunized against with a vaccine that is sprayed into the dog's nostrils. Canine cough is usually included in routine vaccination, but it is often not as effective as the vaccines for other major diseases.

FIVE MONTHS TO ONE YEAR OF AGE
Unless you intend to breed or show your dog, neutering the puppy around six months of age is recommended. Discuss this with your veterinarian. Neutering/spaying has proven to be extremely beneficial to male and female dogs, respectively.

DISEASE REFERENCE CHART

	What is it?	What causes it?	Symptoms
Leptospirosis	Severe disease that affects the internal organs; can be spread to people.	A bacterium, which is often carried by rodents, that enters through mucous membranes and spreads quickly throughout the body.	Range from fever, vomiting and loss of appetite in less severe cases to shock, irreversible kidney damage and possibly death in most severe cases.
Rabies	Potentially deadly virus that infects warm-blooded mammals.	Bite from a carrier of the virus, mainly wild animals.	1st stage: dog exhibits change in behavior, fear. 2nd stage: dog's behavior becomes more aggressive. 3rd stage: loss of coordination, trouble with bodily functions.
Parvovirus	Highly contagious virus, potentially deadly.	Ingestion of the virus, which is usually spread through the feces of infected dogs.	Most common: severe diarrhea. Also vomiting, fatigue, lack of appetite.
Canine cough	Contagious respiratory infection.	Combination of types of bacteria and virus. Most common: *Bordetella bronchiseptica* bacteria and parainfluenza virus.	Chronic cough.
Distemper	Disease primarily affecting respiratory and nervous system.	Virus that is related to the human measles virus.	Mild symptoms such as fever, lack of appetite and mucus secretion progress to evidence of brain damage, "hard pad."
Hepatitis	Virus primarily affecting the liver.	Canine adenovirus type I (CAV-1). Enters system when dog breathes in particles.	Lesser symptoms include listlessness, diarrhea, vomiting. More severe symptoms include "blue-eye" (clumps of virus in eye).
Coronavirus	Virus resulting in digestive problems.	Virus is spread through infected dog's feces.	Stomach upset evidenced by lack of appetite, vomiting, diarrhea.

KNOW WHEN TO POSTPONE A VACCINATION

While the visit to the vet is costly, it is never advisable to update a vaccination when visiting with a sick or pregnant dog. Vaccinations also should be avoided for all elderly dogs. If your dog is showing the signs of any illness or any medical condition, no matter how serious or mild, including skin irritations, do not vaccinate. Likewise, a lame dog should never be vaccinated; any dog undergoing surgery or on any immunosuppressant drugs should not be vaccinated until fully recovered.

Besides eliminating the possibility of pregnancy and pyometra in bitches and testicular cancer in male dogs, it greatly reduces the risk of breast cancer in bitches and prostate cancer in males.

Your vet should provide your puppy with a thorough dental evaluation at six months of age, ascertaining whether all of the permanent teeth have erupted properly. A home dental-care regimen should be initiated at six months, including brushing weekly and providing good dental devices (such as hard plastic or nylon bones). Regular dental care promotes healthy teeth, fresh breath and a longer life.

DOGS OLDER THAN ONE YEAR

Continue to visit the veterinarian at least once a year. There is no such disease as "old age," but bodily functions do change with age. The eyes and ears are no longer as efficient. Liver, kidney and intestinal functions often decline. Proper dietary changes, recommended by your vet, can make life more pleasant for your aging Australian Cattle Dog and you.

SKIN PROBLEMS

Veterinarians are consulted by dog owners for skin problems more than for any other group of diseases or maladies. A dog's skin is as sensitive, if not more so, than human skin, and both can suffer from almost the same ailments (though the occurrence of acne in most dogs is rare). For this reason, veterinary dermatology has developed into a specialty practiced by many vets.

Since many skin problems have visual symptoms that are almost identical, it requires the skill of an experienced veterinary dermatologist to identify and cure many of the more severe skin disorders. Pet shops sell many treatments for skin problems, but most of the treatments are directed at symptoms and not at the underlying problem(s). If your dog is suffering from a skin disorder, you should seek professional assistance as quickly as possible. As with all diseases, the earlier a problem is identified and treated, the more likely it is that the cure will be successful.

HEREDITARY SKIN DISORDERS
Veterinary dermatologists are currently researching a number of skin disorders that are believed to have hereditary bases. These inherited diseases are transmitted by both parents, who appear (phenotypically) normal but have a recessive gene for the disease, meaning that they carry, but are not affected by, the disease. These diseases pose serious problems to breeders because in some instances there are no methods of identifying carriers. Often the secondary diseases associated with these skin conditions are even more debilitating than the skin disorders themselves, including cancers and respiratory problems.

Among the hereditary skin disorders, for which the mode of inheritance is known, are acrodermatitis, cutaneous asthenia (Ehlers-Danlos syndrome), sebaceous adenitis, cyclic hematopoiesis, dermatomyositis, IgA deficiency, color dilution alopecia and nodular dermatofibrosis. Some of these disorders are limited to one or two breeds, while others affect a large number of breeds. All inherited diseases must be diagnosed and treated by a veterinary specialist.

PARASITE BITES
Many of us are allergic to insect bites. The bites itch, erupt and may even become infected. Dogs have the same reaction to fleas, ticks and/or mites. When an insect lands on you, you have the chance to whisk it away with your hand. Unfortunately, when a dog is bitten by a flea, tick or mite, he can only scratch it away or bite it. By the time the dog has been bitten, the parasite has done some of its damage. It may also have laid eggs, which will cause further problems in the near future. The itching from parasite bites is probably due to the saliva injected into the site when the parasite sucks the dog's blood.

A SKUNKY PROBLEM
Have you noticed your dog dragging his rump along the floor? If so, it is likely that his anal sacs are impacted or possibly infected. The anal sacs are small pouches located on both sides of the anus under the skin and muscles. They are about the size and shape of a grape and contain a foul-smelling liquid. Their contents are usually emptied when the dog has a bowel movement but, if not emptied completely, they will impact, which will cause your dog much pain. Fortunately, your veterinarian can tend to this problem easily by draining the sacs for the dog. Be aware that your dog might also empty his anal sacs in cases of extreme fright.

AIRBORNE ALLERGIES

Just as humans suffer from hay fever during the pollinating season, many dogs suffer from the same allergies. When the pollen count is high, your dog might suffer, but don't expect him to sneeze and have a runny nose as a human would. Dogs react to pollen allergies in the same way they react to fleas—they scratch and bite themselves. Dogs, like humans, can be tested for allergens. Discuss the testing with your veterinarian.

AUTO-IMMUNE ILLNESSES

An auto-immune illness is one in which the immune system overacts and does not recognize parts of the affected person; rather, the immune system starts to react as if these parts were foreign and need to be destroyed. An example is rheumatoid arthritis, which occurs when the body does not recognize the joints, thus leading to a very painful and damaging reaction in the joints. This has nothing to do with age, so can occur in children and young dogs. The wear-and-tear arthritis of the older person or dog is known as osteoarthritis.

Lupus is an auto-immune disease that affects dogs as well as people. It can take variable forms, affecting the kidneys, bones and the skin. It can be fatal, so is treated with steroids, which can themselves have very significant side effects. The steroids calm down the allergic reaction to the body's tissues, which helps the lupus, but the steroids also calm down the body's reaction to real foreign substances such as bacteria, and they also thin the skin and bone.

FOOD PROBLEMS

FOOD ALLERGIES

Some dogs can be allergic to many foods that are best-sellers and highly recommended by breeders and veterinarians. Changing the brand of food that you buy may not eliminate the problem if the element to which the dog is allergic is contained in the new brand.

Recognizing a food allergy in a dog can be difficult. Humans often have rashes when they eat foods to which they are allergic, or have swelling of the lips or eyes. Dogs do not usually develop rashes, but react in the same way as they do to an airborne or bite allergy—they itch, scratch and bite. While pollen allergies are usually seasonal, food allergies are year-round problems.

TREATING FOOD ALLERGY

Diagnosis of food allergy is based on a two- to four-week dietary trial with a home-cooked diet fed to the exclusion of all other foods. The diet should consist of boiled rice or potato with a source of protein that the dog has never eaten before, such as fresh or frozen fish, lamb, rabbit or even something as exotic as pheasant if this is available and not too expensive. Water has to be the only drink, and it is really important that no other foods are fed during this trial.

If the dog's condition improves, you will need to try the original diet once again to see if the itching resumes. If it does, then this confirms the diagnosis that the dog is allergic to his original diet. The treatment is long-term feeding of something that does not distress the dog's skin, which may be in the form of one of the commercially available hypoallergenic diets or the homemade diet that you created for the allergy trial.

FOOD INTOLERANCE

Food intolerance is the inability of the dog to completely digest certain foods. This occurs because the dog does not have the chemicals necessary to digest some foodstuffs. These chemicals are called enzymes. All puppies have the enzymes necessary to digest canine milk, but some dogs do not have the enzymes to digest a very different form of milk that is commonly found in human households—milk from cows. In such dogs, drinking cows' milk results in loose bowels, stomach pains and the passage of gas.

Dogs often do not have the enzymes to digest soy or other beans. The treatment is to exclude the foodstuffs that upset your AuCaDo's digestion.

VITAL SIGNS

A dog's normal temperature is 101.5 degrees Fahrenheit. A range of between 100.0 and 102.5 degrees should be considered normal, as each dog's body sets its own temperature. It will be helpful if you take your dog's temperature when you know he is healthy and record it. Then, when you suspect that he is not feeling well, you will have a normal figure to compare the abnormal temperature against.

The normal pulse rate for a dog is between 100 and 125 beats per minute.

A male dog flea, *Ctenocephalides canis.*

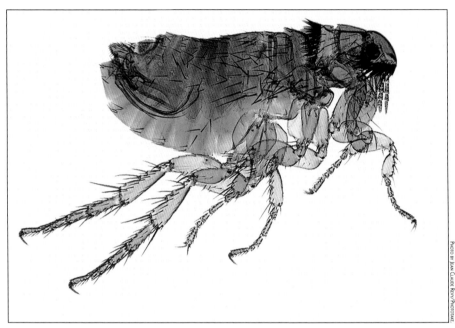

PHOTO BY JEAN CLAUDE REVY/PHOTOTAKE

EXTERNAL PARASITES

FLEAS

Of all the problems to which dogs are prone, none is more well known and frustrating than fleas. Flea infestation is relatively simple to cure but difficult to prevent. Parasites that are harbored inside the body are a bit more difficult to eradicate but they are easier to control.

To control flea infestation, you have to understand the flea's life cycle. Fleas are often thought of as a summertime problem, but centrally heated homes have changed the patterns and fleas can be found at any time of the year. The most effective method of flea control is a two-stage approach: one stage to kill the adult fleas, and the other to control the development of pre-adult fleas. Unfortunately, no single active ingredient is effective against all stages of the life cycle.

FLEA KILLER CAUTION—"POISON"

Flea-killers are poisonous. You should not spray these toxic chemicals on areas of a dog's body that he licks, including his genitals and his face. Flea killers taken internally are a better answer, but check with your vet in case internal therapy is not advised for your dog.

Life Cycle Stages

During its life, a flea will pass through four life stages: egg, larva, pupa or nymph and adult. The adult stage is the most visible and irritating stage of the flea life cycle, and this is why the majority of flea-control products concentrate on this stage. The fact is that adult fleas account for only 1% of the total flea population, and the other 99% exist in pre-adult stages, i.e., eggs, larvae and nymphs. The pre-adult stages are barely visible to the naked eye.

The Life Cycle of the Flea

Eggs are laid on the dog, usually in quantities of about 20 or 30, several times a day. The adult female flea must have a blood meal before each egg-laying session. When first laid, the eggs will cling to the dog's hair, as the eggs are still moist. However, they will quickly dry out and fall from the dog, especially if the dog moves around or scratches. Many eggs will fall off in the dog's favorite area or an area in which he spends a lot of time, such as his bed.

Once the eggs fall from the dog onto the carpet or furniture, they will hatch into larvae. This takes from one to ten days. Larvae are not particularly mobile and will usually travel only a few inches from where they hatch. However, they do have a tendency to move away from bright light and heavy

**EN GARDE:
CATCHING FLEAS OFF GUARD!**
Consider the following ways to arm yourself against fleas:
- Add a small amount of pennyroyal or eucalyptus oil to your dog's bath. These natural remedies repel fleas.
- Supplement your dog's food with fresh garlic (minced or grated) and a hearty amount of brewer's yeast, both of which ward off fleas.
- Use a flea comb on your dog daily. Submerge fleas in a cup of bleach to kill them quickly.
- Confine the dog to only a few rooms to limit the spread of fleas in the home.
- Vacuum daily...and get all of the crevices! Dispose of the bag every few days until the problem is under control.
- Wash your dog's bedding daily. Cover cushions where your dog sleeps with towels, and wash the towels often.

traffic—under furniture and behind doors are common places to find high quantities of flea larvae.

The flea larvae feed on dead organic matter, including adult flea feces, until they are ready to change into adult fleas. Fleas will usually remain as larvae for around seven days. After this period, the larvae will pupate into protective pupae. While inside the pupae, the larvae will undergo metamorphosis and change into

Fleas have been measured as being able to jump 300,000 times and can jump over 150 times their length in any direction, including straight up.

adult fleas. This can take as little time as a few days, but the adult fleas can remain inside the pupae waiting to hatch for up to two years. The pupae are signaled to hatch by certain stimuli, such as physical pressure—the pupae's being stepped on, heat from an animal's lying on the pupae or increased carbon-dioxide levels and vibrations—indicating that a suitable host is available.

Once hatched, the adult flea must feed within a few days. Once the adult flea finds a host, it will not leave voluntarily. It only becomes dislodged by grooming or the host animal's scratching. The adult flea will remain on the

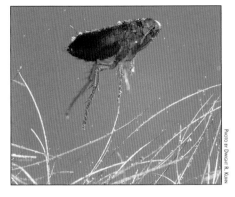

host for the duration of its life unless forcibly removed.

TREATING THE ENVIRONMENT AND THE DOG

Treating fleas should be a two-pronged attack. First, the environment needs to be treated; this includes carpets and furniture, especially the dog's bedding and areas underneath furniture. The environment should be treated with a household spray containing an Insect Growth Regulator (IGR) and an insecticide to kill the adult fleas. Most IGRs are effective against eggs and larvae; they actually mimic the fleas' own hormones and stop the eggs and larvae from developing into adult fleas. There are currently no treatments available to attack the pupa stage of the life cycle, so the adult insecticide is used to kill the newly hatched adult fleas before they find a host. Most IGRs are active for many months, while adult insecticides are only active

A scanning electron micrograph of a dog or cat flea, *Ctenocephalides*, magnified more than 100x. This image has been colorized for effect.

THE LIFE CYCLE OF THE FLEA

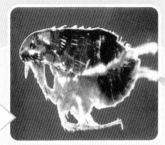

Adult

**Pupa
or
Nymph**

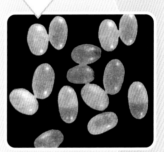

Egg

Larva

Fleas have been around for millions of years and have adapted to changing host animals. They are able to go through a complete life cycle in less than one month or they can extend their lives to almost two years by remaining as pupae or cocoons. They do not need blood or any other food for up to 20 months.

INSECT GROWTH REGULATOR (IGR)

Two types of products should be used when treating fleas—a product to treat the pet and a product to treat the home. Adult fleas represent less than 1% of the flea population. The pre-adult fleas (eggs, larvae and pupae) represent more than 99% of the flea population and are found in the environment; it is in the case of pre-adult fleas that products containing an Insect Growth Regulator (IGR) should be used in the home.

IGRs are a new class of compounds used to prevent the development of insects. They do not kill the insect outright, but instead use the insect's biology against it to stop it from completing its growth. Products that contain methoprene are the world's first and leading IGRs. Used to control fleas and other insects, this type of IGR will stop flea larvae from developing and protect the house for up to seven months.

The American dog tick, Dermacentor variabilis, is probably the most common tick found on dogs. Look at the strength in its eight legs! No wonder it's hard to detach them.

is to apply an adult insecticide to the dog. Traditionally, this would be in the form of a collar or a spray, but more recent innovations include digestible insecticides that poison the fleas when they ingest the dog's blood. Alternatively, there are drops that, when placed on the back of the dog's neck, spread throughout the hair and skin to kill adult fleas.

TICKS

Though not as common as fleas, ticks are found all over the tropical and temperate world. They don't bite, like fleas; they harpoon. They dig their sharp proboscis (nose) into the dog's skin and drink the blood. Their only food and drink is dog's for a few days.

When treating with a household spray, it is a good idea to vacuum before applying the product. This stimulates as many pupae as possible to hatch into adult fleas. The vacuum cleaner should also be treated with an insecticide to prevent the eggs and larvae that have been collected in the vacuum bag from hatching.

The second stage of treatment

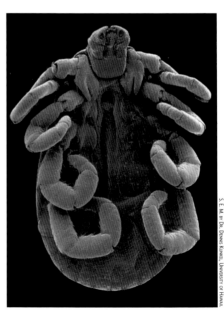

blood. Dogs can get Lyme disease, Rocky Mountain spotted fever, tick bite paralysis and many other diseases from ticks. They may live where fleas are found and they like to hide in cracks or seams in walls. They are controlled the same way fleas are controlled.

The American dog tick, *Dermacentor variabilis*, may well be the most common dog tick in many geographical areas, especially those areas where the climate is hot and humid. Most dog ticks have life expectancies of a week to six months, depending upon climatic conditions. They can neither jump nor fly, but they can crawl slowly and can range up to 16 feet to reach a sleeping or unsuspecting dog.

MITES

Just as fleas and ticks can be problematic for your dog, mites can also lead to an itchy nuisance. Microscopic in size, mites are related to ticks and generally take up permanent residence on their host animal—in this case, your dog! The term *mange* refers to any infestation caused by one of the mighty mites, of which there are six varieties that concern dog owners.

Demodex mites cause a condition known as demodicosis (sometimes called red mange or

DEER-TICK CROSSING
The great outdoors may be fun for your dog, but it also is a home to dangerous ticks. Deer ticks carry a bacterium known as *Borrelia burgdorferi* and are most active in the autumn and spring. When infections are caught early, penicillin and tetracycline are effective antibiotics, but, if left untreated, the bacteria may cause neurological, kidney and cardiac problems as well as long-term trouble with walking and painful joints.

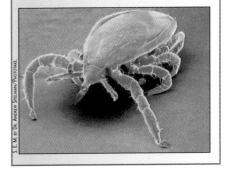

S.E.M. BY DR. ANDREW SPIELMAN/PHOTOTAKE.

PHOTO BY DR. DENNIS KUNKEL, UNIVERSITY OF HAWAII.

The head of an American dog tick, *Dermacentor variabilis*, enlarged and colorized for effect.

The mange mite, *Psoroptes bovis,* can infest cattle and other domestic animals.

PHOTO BY JAMES HAYDEN/YDAW/PHOTOTAKE.

follicular mange), in which the mites live in the dog's hair follicles and sebaceous glands in larger-than-normal numbers. This type of mange is commonly passed from the dam to her puppies and usually shows up on the puppies' muzzles, though demodicosis is not transferable from one normal dog to another. Most dogs recover from this type of mange without any treatment, though topical therapies are commonly prescribed by the vet.

The *Cheyletiellosis* mite is the hook-mouthed culprit associated with "walking dandruff," a condition that affects dogs as well as cats and rabbits. This mite lives on the surface of the animal's skin and is readily transferable through direct or indirect contact with an affected animal. The dandruff is present in the form of scaly skin, which may or may not be itchy. If not treated, this mange can affect a whole kennel of dogs and can be spread to humans as well.

The *Sarcoptes* mite causes intense itching on the dog in the form of a condition known as scabies or sarcoptic mange. The cycle of the *Sarcoptes* mite lasts about three weeks, and the mites live in the top layer of the dog's skin (epidermis), preferably in

Human lice look like dog lice; the two are closely related.

PHOTO BY DWIGHT R. KUHN.

areas with little hair. Scabies is highly contagious and can be passed to humans. Sometimes an allergic reaction to the mite worsens the severe itching associated with sarcoptic mange.

Ear mites, *Otodectes cynotis,* lead to otodectic mange, which most commonly affects the outer ear canal of the dog, though other areas can be affected as well. Dogs with ear-mite infestation commonly scratch at their ears, causing further irritation, and shake their heads. Dark brown droppings in the outer ear confirm the diagnosis. Your vet can prescribe a treatment to flush out the ears and kill any eggs in the ears. A complete month of treatment is necessary to cure the mange.

Two other mites, less common in dogs, include *Dermanyssus gallinae* (the poultry or red mite) and *Eutrombicula alfreddugesi* (the North American mite associated with trombiculidiasis or chigger infestation). The poultry mite frequently lives on chickens, but can transfer to dogs who spend time near farm animals. Chigger infestation affects dogs in the

---

DO NOT MIX

Never mix parasite-control products without first consulting your vet. Some products can become toxic when combined with others and can cause fatal consequences.

NOT A DROP TO DRINK

Never allow your dog to swim in polluted water or public areas where water quality can be suspect. Even perfectly clear water can harbor parasites, many of which can cause serious to fatal illnesses in canines. Areas inhabited by waterfowl and other wildlife are especially dangerous.

---

central US who have exposure to woodlands. The types of mange caused by both of these mites are treatable by vets.

INTERNAL PARASITES

Most animals—fishes, birds and mammals, including dogs and humans—have worms and other parasites that live inside their bodies. According to Dr. Herbert R. Axelrod, the fish pathologist, there are two kinds of parasites: dumb and smart. The smart parasites live in peaceful cooperation with their hosts (symbiosis), while the dumb parasites kill their hosts. Most worm infections are relatively easy to control. If they are not controlled, they weaken the host dog to the point that other medical problems occur, but they do not kill the host as dumb parasites would.

A brown dog tick, *Rhipicephalus sanguineus,* is an uncommon but annoying tick found on dogs.
PHOTO BY CAROLINA BIOLOGICAL SUPPLY/PHOTOTAKE.

PHOTO BY CAROLINA BIOLOGICAL SUPPLY/PHOTOTAKE.

The roundworm *Rhabditis* can infect both dogs and humans.

ROUNDWORMS

Average-size dogs can pass 1,360,000 roundworm eggs every day. For example, if there were only 1 million dogs in the world, the world would be saturated with thousands of tons of dog feces. These feces would contain around 15,000,000,000 roundworm eggs.

Up to 31% of home yards and children's sand boxes in the US contain roundworm eggs.

Flushing dog's feces down the toilet is not a safe practice because the usual sewage treatments do not destroy roundworm eggs.

Infected puppies start shedding roundworm eggs at three weeks of age. They can be infected by their mother's milk.

The roundworm, *Ascaris lumbricoides.*

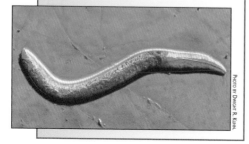

PHOTO BY DWIGHT R. KUHN.

ROUNDWORMS

The roundworms that infect dogs are known scientifically as *Toxocara canis.* They live in the dog's intestines and shed eggs continually. It has been estimated that a dog produces about 6 or more ounces of feces every day. Each ounce of feces averages hundreds of thousands of roundworm eggs. There are no known areas in which dogs roam that do not contain roundworm eggs. The greatest danger of roundworms is that they infect people, too! It is wise to have your dog tested regularly for roundworms.

In young puppies, roundworms cause bloated bellies, diarrhea, coughing and vomiting, and are transmitted from the dam (through blood or milk). Affected puppies will not appear as animated as normal puppies. The worms appear spaghetti-like, measuring as long as 6 inches. Adult dogs can acquire roundworms through coprophagia (eating contaminated feces) or by killing rodents that carry roundworms.

Roundworm infection can kill puppies and cause severe problems in adults, as the hatched larvae travel to the lungs and trachea through the bloodstream. Cleanliness is the best preventative for roundworms. Always pick up after your dog and dispose of feces in appropriate receptacles.

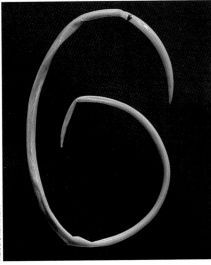

PHOTO BY DWIGHT R. KUHN.

HOOKWORMS

In the United States, dog owners have to be concerned about four different species of hookworm, the most common and most serious of which is *Ancylostoma caninum*, which prefers warm climates. The others are *Ancylostoma braziliense*, *Ancylostoma tubaeforme* and *Uncinaria stenocephala*, the latter of which is a concern to dogs living in the northern US and Canada, as this species prefers cold climates.

Hookworms are dangerous to humans as well as to dogs and cats, and can be the cause of severe anemia due to iron deficiency. The worm uses its teeth to attach itself to the dog's intestines and changes the site of its attachment about six times per day. Each time the worm reposi-

tions itself, the dog loses blood and can become anemic. *Ancylostoma caninum* is the most likely of the four species to cause anemia in the dog.

Symptoms of hookworm infection include dark stools, weight loss, general weakness, pale coloration and anemia, as well as possible skin problems. Fortunately, hookworms are easily purged from the affected dog with a number of medications that have proven effective. Discuss these with your vet. Most heartworm preventatives include a hookworm insecticide as well.

Owners also must be aware that hookworms can infect humans, who can acquire the larvae through exposure to contaminated feces. Since the worms cannot complete their life cycle on a human, the worms simply infest the skin and cause irritation. This condition is known as cutaneous larva migrans syndrome. As a preventative, use disposable gloves or a "poop-scoop" to pick up your dog's droppings and prevent your dog (or neighborhood cats) from defecating in children's play areas.

The hookworm, *Ancylostoma caninum*.

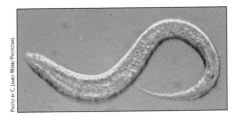

PHOTO BY C. JAMES WEBB/PHOTOTAKE.

The infective stage of the hookworm larva.

TAPEWORMS

Humans, rats, squirrels, foxes, coyotes, wolves and domestic dogs are all susceptible to tapeworm infection. Except in humans, tapeworms are usually not a fatal infection. Infected individuals can harbor 1000 parasitic worms.

Tapeworms, like some other types of worm, are hermaphroditic, meaning male and female in the same worm.

If dogs eat infected rats or mice, or anything else infected with tapeworm, they get the tapeworm disease. One month after attaching to a dog's intestine, the worm starts shedding eggs. These eggs are infective immediately. Infective eggs can live for a few months without a host animal.

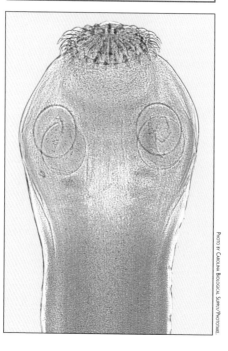

The head and rostellum (the round prominence on the scolex) of a tapeworm, which infects dogs and humans.

PHOTO BY CAROLINA BIOLOGICAL SUPPLY/PHOTOTAKE

TAPEWORMS

There are many species of tapeworm, all of which are carried by fleas! The most common tapeworm affecting dogs is known as *Dipylidium caninum*. The dog eats the flea and starts the tapeworm cycle. Humans can also be infected with tapeworms—so don't eat fleas! Fleas are so small that your dog could pass them onto your hands, your plate or your food and thus make it possible for you to ingest a flea that is carrying tapeworm eggs.

While tapeworm infection is not life-threatening in dogs (smart parasite!), it can be the cause of a very serious liver disease for humans. About 50% of the humans infected with *Echinococcus multilocularis*, a type of tapeworm that causes alveolar hydatid, perish.

WHIPWORMS

In North America, whipworms are counted among the most common parasitic worms in dogs. The whipworm's scientific name is *Trichuris vulpis*. These worms attach themselves in the lower parts of the intestine, where they feed. Affected dogs may only experience upset tummies, colic and diarrhea. These worms, however, can live for months or years in the dog, beginning their larval stage in the small intestine, spending their adult stage in the large intestine and finally passing infective eggs through the dog's feces. The only way to detect whipworms is through a fecal examination, though this is not always foolproof. Treatment for whipworms is tricky, due to the worms' unusual life-cycle pattern, and very often dogs are reinfected due to exposure to infective eggs on the ground. The whipworm eggs can survive in the environment for as long as five years; thus, cleaning up droppings in your own backyard as well as in public places is absolutely essential for sanitation purposes and the health of your dog and others.

THREADWORMS

Though less common than roundworms, hookworms and those previously mentioned, threadworms concern dog owners in the southwestern US and Gulf Coast area where the climate is hot and humid. Living in the small intestine of the dog, this worm measures a mere 2 millimeters and is round in shape. Like that of the whipworm, the threadworm's life cycle is very complex and the eggs and larvae are passed through the feces. A deadly disease in humans, *Strongyloides* readily infects people, and the handling of feces is the most common means of transmission. Threadworms are most often seen in young puppies; bloody diarrhea and pneumonia are symptoms. Sick puppies must be isolated and treated immediately; vets recommend a follow-up treatment one month later.

HEARTWORM PREVENTATIVES

There are many heartworm preventatives on the market, many of which are sold at your veterinarian's office. These products can be given daily or monthly, depending on the manufacturer's instructions. All of these preventatives contain chemical insecticides directed at killing heartworms, which leads to some controversy among dog owners. In effect, heartworm preventatives are necessary evils, though you should determine how necessary based on your pet's lifestyle. There is no doubt that heartworm is a dreadful disease that threatens the lives of dogs. However, the likelihood of your dog's being bitten by an infected mosquito is slim in most places, and a mosquito-repellent (or an herbal remedy such as Wormwood or Black Walnut) is much safer for your dog and will not compromise his immune system (the way heartworm preventatives will). Should you decide to use the traditional preventative "medications," you can consider giving the pill every other or third month. Since the toxins in the pill will kill the heartworms at all stages of development, the pill would be effective in killing larvae, nymphs or adults, and it takes four months for the larvae to reach the adult stage. Thus, there is no rationale to poisoning the dog's system on a monthly basis. Lastly, do not give the pill during the winter months since there are no mosquitoes around to pass on their infection, unless you live in a tropical environment.

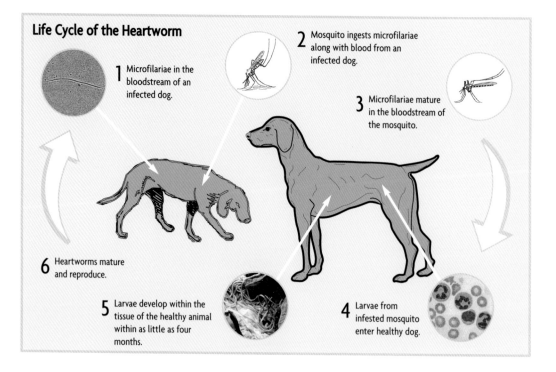

Life Cycle of the Heartworm

1 Microfilariae in the bloodstream of an infected dog.

2 Mosquito ingests microfilariae along with blood from an infected dog.

3 Microfilariae mature in the bloodstream of the mosquito.

4 Larvae from infested mosquito enter healthy dog.

5 Larvae develop within the tissue of the healthy animal within as little as four months.

6 Heartworms mature and reproduce.

HEARTWORMS

Heartworms are thin, extended worms up to 12 inches long, which live in a dog's heart and the major blood vessels surrounding it. Dogs may have up to 200 worms. Symptoms may be loss of energy, loss of appetite, coughing, the development of a pot belly and anemia.

Heartworms are transmitted by mosquitoes. The mosquito drinks the blood of an infected dog and takes in larvae with the blood. The larvae, called microfilariae, develop within the body of the mosquito and are passed on to the next dog bitten after the larvae mature. It takes two to three weeks for the larvae to develop to the infective stage within the body of the mosquito. Dogs are usually treated at about six weeks of age and maintained on a prophylactic dose given monthly.

Blood testing for heartworms is not necessarily indicative of how seriously your dog is infected. Although this is a dangerous disease, it is not easy for a dog to be infected. Discuss the various preventatives with your vet, as there are many different types now available. Together you can decide on a safe course of prevention for your dog.

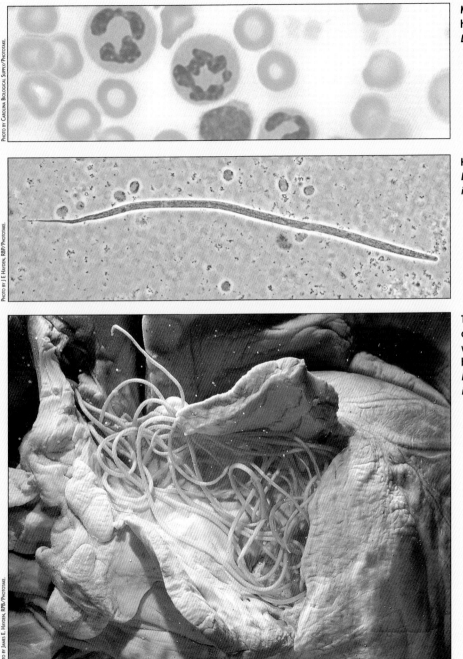

Magnified heartworm larvae, *Dirofilaria immitis.*

Heartworm, *Dirofilaria immitis.*

The heart of a dog infected with canine heartworm, *Dirofilaria immitis.*

AUSTRALIAN CATTLE DOG

When you purchase your Australian Cattle Dog, you will make it clear to the breeder whether you want one just as a family companion and pet, or if you hope to be buying an Australian Cattle Dog with show prospects. No reputable breeder will sell you a young puppy and tell you that it is *definitely* of show quality, for so much can go wrong during the early months of a puppy's development. If you plan to show, what you will hopefully have acquired is a puppy with "show potential."

To the novice, exhibiting an AuCaDo in the show ring may look easy, but it takes a lot of hard work and devotion to do top winning at a show such as the prestigious Westminster Kennel Club dog show, not to mention a little luck, too!

The first concept that the canine novice learns when watching a dog show is that each dog first competes against members of his own breed. Once the judge has selected the best member of each breed (Best of Breed), provided that the show is judged on a Group system, that chosen dog will compete with other dogs in his group. Finally,

the dogs chosen first in each group will compete for Best in Show.

The second concept that you must understand is that the dogs are not actually compared against one another. The judge compares each dog against his breed standard, the written description of the ideal specimen that is approved by the American Kennel Club (AKC). While some early breed standards were indeed based on specific dogs that were famous or popular, many dedicated enthusiasts say that a perfect specimen, as described in the standard, has never walked into a show ring, has never been bred and, to the woe of dog breeders around the globe, does not exist. Breeders attempt to get as close to this ideal as possible with every litter, but theoretically the "perfect" dog is so elusive that it is impossible. (And if the "perfect" dog were born, breeders and judges would never agree that it was indeed "perfect.")

If you are interested in exploring the world of dog showing, your best bet is to join your local breed club or the national parent club, which is the Australian Cattle Dog Club of

Aust. Ch. Kombinalong Super "K," winning one of his many specialty Bests in Show with the Herding Group specialist Dr. Robert Zammit.

America. These clubs often host both regional and national specialties, shows only for Australian Cattle Dogs, which can include conformation as well as obedience, herding and other types of trials. Even if you have no intention of competing with your AuCaDo, a specialty is like a festival for lovers of the breed who congregate to share their favorite topic: the Australian Cattle Dog! Clubs also send out newsletters, and some organize training days and seminars in order that people may learn more about their chosen breed. To locate the breed club closest to you, contact the American Kennel Club, which furnishes the rules and regulations for all of these events plus general dog registration and other basic requirements of dog ownership.

The American Kennel Club offers three kinds of conformation shows: an all-breed show (for all AKC-recognized breeds), a specialty show (for one breed only, usually sponsored by the parent club) and a Group show (for all breeds in the group).

For a dog to become an AKC champion of record, the dog must accumulate 15 points at the shows from at least three different judges, including two "majors." A "major" is defined as a three-, four- or five-point win, and the number of points per win is determined by the number of dogs entered in the show on that day. Depending on the breed, the number of points that are awarded varies. More dogs are needed to rack up the points in more popular breeds, and less dogs are needed in less numerous breeds. The Australian Cattle Dog attracts modest numbers at all-breed shows.

At any dog show, only one dog and one bitch of each breed can win points. Dog showing does not offer "co-ed" classes. Dogs and bitches never compete against each other in the classes. Non-champion dogs are called "class dogs" because they compete in one of five classes. Dogs are entered in a particular class

---

CLUB CONTACTS

You can get information about dog shows from the national kennel clubs:

American Kennel Club
5580 Centerview Dr., Raleigh, NC 27606-3390
www.akc.org

United Kennel Club
100 E. Kilgore Road, Kalamazoo, MI 49002
www.ukcdogs.com

Canadian Kennel Club
89 Skyway Ave., Suite 100, Etobicoke, Ontario
M9W 6R4, Canada
www.ckc.ca

The Kennel Club
1-5 Clarges St., Piccadilly, London
W1Y 8AB, UK
www.the-kennel-club.org.uk

Cattle Dogs must be trained to tolerate being handled by strangers. Dog show judges go over each dog with their hands to assess the dogs' physical construction.

MEETING THE IDEAL

The American Kennel Club defines a standard as: "A description of the ideal dog of each recognized breed, to serve as an ideal against which dogs are judged at shows." This "blueprint" is drawn up by the breed's recognized parent club, approved by a majority of its membership and then submitted to the AKC for approval.

The AKC states that "An understanding of any breed must begin with its standard. This applies to all dogs, not just those intended for showing." The picture that the standard draws of the dog's type, gait, temperament and structure is the guiding image used by breeders as they plan their programs.

The judge at the show begins judging the Puppy Class, first dogs and then bitches, and proceeds through the classes. The judge places his winners first through fourth in each class. In the Winners Class, the first-place winners of each class compete with one another to determine Winners Dog and Winners Bitch. The judge also places a Reserve Winners Dog and Reserve Winners Bitch, which could be awarded the points in the case of a disqualification. The Winners Dog and Winners Bitch are the two that are awarded the points for the breed, then compete with any champions of record (often called "specials") entered in the show. The judge reviews the Winners Dog, Winners Bitch and all of the champions to select his Best of Breed. The Best of Winners is selected between the Winners Dog and Winners Bitch. Were one of these two to be selected Best of Breed, he or she would automatically be named Best of Winners as well. Finally the judge selects his Best of Opposite Sex to the Best of Breed winner.

At a Group show or all-breed show, the Best of Breed winners from each breed then compete against one another for Group One through Group Four. The judge compares each Best of Breed to his breed standard, and the dog that most closely lives up to the ideal for his breed is selected as

depending on age and previous show wins. To begin, there is the Puppy Class (for 6- to 9-month-olds and for 9- to 12-month-olds); this class is followed by the Novice Class (for dogs that have not won any first prizes except in the Puppy Class or three first prizes in the Novice Class and have not accumulated any points toward their champion title); the Bred-by-Exhibitor Class (for dogs handled by their breeders or by one of the breeder's immediate family); the American-bred Class (for dogs bred in the US) and the Open Class (for any dog that is not a champion).

The AuCaDo's gait is of utmost importance, as a dog with atypical movement would not be able to perform the breed's intended funtion. This dog moves confidently around the ring.

Group One. Finally, all seven group winners (from the Herding Group, Toy Group, Hound Group, etc.) compete for Best in Show.

To find out about dog shows in your area, you can subscribe to the AKC's monthly magazine, the *American Kennel Gazette*, and the accompanying *Events Calendar*. You can also look in your local newspaper for advertisements for dog shows in your area or go on the Internet to the AKC's website, www.akc.org.

If your AuCaDo is six months of age or older and registered with the AKC, you can enter him in a dog show where the breed is offered classes. Provided that your Australian Cattle Dog does not have a disqualifying fault, he can compete. Only unaltered dogs can be entered in a dog show, so if you have spayed or neutered your AuCaDo, your dog cannot compete in conformation shows. The reason for this is simple. Dog shows are the main forum to

WESTMINSTER KENNEL CLUB DOG SHOW

BUD LIGHT

RING 5

RING 6

RING 7

The world's oldest dog show is the Westminster Kennel Club Dog Show, which takes place annually in New York City. The Group finals are completely televised, and the show has an attendance of more than 50,000 people per day.

prove which representatives in a breed are worthy of being bred. Only dogs that have achieved championships—the AKC "seal of approval" for quality in pure-bred dogs—should be bred. Altered dogs, however, can participate in other AKC events such as obedience trials and the Canine Good Citizen® program.

Before you actually step into the ring, you would be well advised to sit back and observe the judge's ring procedure. If it is your first time in the ring, do not be over-anxious and run to the front of the line. It is much better to stand back and study how the exhibitor in front of you is performing. The judge asks each handler to "stack" the dog, hopefully showing the dog off to his best advantage. The judge will observe the dog from a distance and from different angles, and approach the dog to check his teeth, overall structure, alertness and muscle tone, as well as consider how well the dog "conforms" to the standard. Most importantly, the judge will have the exhibitor move the dog around the ring in some pattern that he should specify (another advantage to not going first, but always listen since some judges change their directions—and the judge is always right!). Finally, the judge will give the dog one last look before moving on to the next exhibitor.

If you are not in the top four in your class at your first show, do not be discouraged. Be patient and consistent, and you may eventually find yourself in a winning line-up. Remember that the winners were once in your shoes and have devoted many hours and much money to earn the placement. If you find that your dog is losing every time and never getting a nod, it may be time to consider a different dog sport or to just enjoy your AuCaDo as a pet. Parent clubs offer other events, such as agility, herding events, obedience, instinct tests and more, which may be of interest to the owner of a well-trained Australian Cattle Dog.

OBEDIENCE TRIALS
Obedience trials in the US trace back to the early 1930s when organized obedience training was developed to demonstrate how well dog and owner could work

An AuCaDo takes a well-deserved break from the hustle and bustle of a show.

Multi-BISS and Royal CC winner Ch. Kombinalong C'est Super with breeder/owner/handler Narelle Hammond-Robertson.

together. The pioneer of obedience trials is Mrs. Helen Whitehouse Walker, a Standard Poodle fancier, who designed a series of exercises after the Associated Sheep, Police, Army Dog Society of Great Britain. Since the days of Mrs. Walker, obedience trials have grown by leaps and bounds, and today there are over 2,000 trials held in the US every year, with more than 100,000 dogs competing. Any AKC-registered dog can enter an obedience trial, regardless of conformational disqualifications or neutering.

Obedience trials are divided into three levels of progressive difficulty. At the first level, the Novice, dogs compete for the title Companion Dog (CD); at the intermediate level, the Open, dogs compete for the title Companion Dog Excellent (CDX); and at the advanced level, the Utility, dogs compete for the title Utility Dog (UD). Classes are sub-divided into "A" (for beginners) and "B" (for more experienced handlers). A perfect score at any level is 200, and a dog must score 170 or better to earn a "leg," of which three are needed to earn the title. To earn points, the dog must score more than 50% of the available points in each exercise; the possible points range from 20 to 40.

Each level consists of a different set of exercises. In the Novice level, the dog must heel on- and off-lead, come, long sit, long down and stand for examination. These skills are the basic ones required for a well-behaved "Companion Dog." The Open level requires that the dog perform the same exercises as in the Novice, but without a leash for extended lengths of time, as well as retrieve a dumbbell, broad jump and drop on recall. In the Utility level, dogs must perform ten difficult exercises, including scent discrimination, hand signals for basic commands, directed jump and directed retrieve.

Once a dog has earned the UD title, he can compete with other proven obedience dogs for the coveted title of Utility Dog Excellent (UDX), which requires that the dog win "legs" in ten shows. Utility Dogs who earn "legs" in Open B and Utility B earn points toward their Obedience Trial Champion title. In 1977, the title Obedience Trial Champion (OTCh.) was established by the AKC. To become an OTCh., a dog needs to earn 100 points, which requires three first places in Open B and Utility under three different judges.

The Grand Prix of obedience trials, the AKC National Obedience Invitational gives qualifying Utility Dogs the chance to win the newest and highest title: National Obedience Champion (NOC). Only the top 25 ranked obedience dogs, plus any dog ranked in the top 3 in his breed, are allowed to compete.

AGILITY TRIALS

Having had its origins in the UK back in 1977, agility had its official AKC beginning in the US in August 1994, when the first licensed agility trials were held. The AKC allows all registered breeds (including Miscellaneous Class breeds) to participate, providing the dog is 12 months of age or older. Agility is designed so that the handler demonstrates how well the dog can work at his side. The handler directs his dog over an obstacle course that includes jumps as well as tires, the dog walk, weave poles, pipe tunnels, collapsed tunnels, etc. While working his way through

TEMPERAMENT PLUS

Although it seems that physical conformation is the only factor considered in the show ring, temperament is also of utmost importance. An aggressive or fearful dog should not be shown, as bad behavior will not be tolerated and may pose a threat to the judge, other exhibitors, you and your dog.

The judge reviews the line of competitors while the handlers "stack" the dogs to look their best.

the course, the dog must keep one eye and ear on the handler and the rest of his body on the course. The handler gives verbal and hand signals to guide the dog through the course.

The first organization to promote agility trials in the US was the United States Dog Agility Association, Inc. (USDAA), which was established in 1986 and spawned numerous member clubs around the country. Both the USDAA and the AKC offer titles to winning dogs. Three titles are available through the USDAA: Agility Dog (AD), Advanced Agility Dog (AAD) and Master Agility Dog (MAD). The AKC offers Novice Agility (NA), Open Agility (OA), Agility Excellent (AX) and Master Agility Excellent (MX). Beyond these four AKC titles, dogs can win additional ones in "jumper" classes, Jumpers with Weave Novice (NAJ), Open (OAJ) and Excellent (MXJ), which lead to the ultimate title(s): MACH, Master Agility Champion. Dogs can continue to add number designations to the MACH titles, indicating how many times the dog has met the MACH requirements, such as MACH1, MACH2 and so on.

Agility is great fun for dog and owner with many rewards for everyone involved. Interested owners should join a training club that has obstacles and experi-

A GENTLEMAN'S SPORT

Whether or not your dog wins top honors, showing is a pleasant social event. Sometimes, one may meet a troublemaker or nasty exhibitor, but these people should be ignored and forgotten. In the extremely rare case that someone threatens or harasses you or your dog, you can lodge a complaint with the hosting kennel club. This should be done with extreme prudence. Complaints are investigated seriously and should never be filed on a whim.

enced agility handlers who can introduce you and your dog to the "ropes" (and tires, tunnels, etc.).

TRACKING

Any dog is capable of tracking, using his nose to follow a trail. Tracking tests are exciting and competitive ways to test your Australian Cattle Dog's scenting ability. The AKC started tracking tests in 1937, when the first AKC-licensed test took place as part of the Utility level at an obedience trial. Ten years later in 1947, the AKC offered the first title, Tracking Dog (TD). It was not until 1980 that the AKC added the title Tracking Dog Excellent (TDX), which was followed by the title Versatile Surface Tracking (VST) in 1995. The title Champion Tracker (CT) is awarded to a dog who has earned all three titles.

In the beginning level of tracking, the owner follows the dog through a field on a long lead. To earn the TD title, the dog must follow a track laid by a human 30 to 120 minutes prior. The track is about 500 yards with up to 5 directional changes. The TDX requires that the dog follow a track that is 3 to 5 hours old over a course up to 1,000 yards with up to 7 directional changes. The VST requires that the dog follow a track up to 5 hours old through an urban setting.

HERDING EVENTS

The first recorded sheepdog trial was held in Wales in the late 19th century and, since then, the popularity of herding events has grown around the world. The AKC began offering herding events in 1989, and participation is open to all breeds in the Herding Group as well as Rottweilers and Samoyeds. These events are designed to evaluate the dogs' herding instincts, and the aim is to develop these innate skills and show that herding dogs today can still perform the functions for which they were originally intended, whether or not they are actually used in working capacities.

Herding events are designed to simulate farm situations and are held on two levels: tests and trials. AKC herding tests are more basic and are scored on a pass/fail system, meaning that dogs do not compete against each other to earn titles. Titles at this level are Herding Tested (HT) and the more difficult Pre-Trial Tested (PT). From herding tests, dogs can move on to the more challenging trial level.

Herding trials are competitive and require more training and experience. There are three different courses (A, B and C, each with a different type of farm situation) with different types of livestock (cattle, sheep or ducks). There are three titles available on each course, Herding Started, Herding Intermediate and Herding Advanced, with each level being progressively more difficult.

Handlers can choose the type of course and type of livestock for their dogs; obviously, as its name implies, the Australian Cattle Dog works cattle best. Once an Advanced title has been earned on a course, the dog can then begin to strive for the Herding Champion title.

In addition to events held by the AKC, breed clubs often hold herding events for the AuCaDo. Other organizations, such as the American Herding Breed Association and the Australian Shepherd Club of America, hold trials that are open to all herding breeds; the organization of these events and the titles awarded differ from those of the AKC.

The dog-handler relationship plays a big role in a dog's success at shows.

AUSTRALIAN CATTLE DOG

As an Australian Cattle Dog owner, you have selected your dog so that you and your loved ones can have a companion, a protector, a friend and a four-legged family member. You invest time, money and effort to care for and train the family's new charge. Of course, this chosen canine behaves perfectly! Well, perfectly like a *dog*.

THINK LIKE A DOG

Dogs do not think like humans, nor do humans think like dogs, though we try. Unfortunately, a dog is incapable of compre-hending how humans think, so the responsibility falls on the owner to adopt a viable canine mindset. Dogs cannot rationalize, and they exist in the present moment. Many a dog owner makes the mistake in training of thinking that he can reprimand his dog for something the dog did a while ago. Basically, you cannot even reprimand a dog for something he did 20 seconds ago! Either catch him in the act or forget it! It is a waste of your and your dog's time—in his mind, you are reprimanding him for whatever he is doing at that moment.

The following behavioral problems represent some which owners most commonly encounter. Every dog is unique and every situation is unique. No author could purport for you to solve your Australian Cattle Dog's problems simply by reading a chapter in a breed book. Here we outline some basic "dogspeak" so that owners' chances of solving behavioral problems are increased. Discuss bad habits with your veterinarian and he can recommend a behavioral specialist to consult in appropriate cases.

Since behavioral abnormali-ties are the main reason for owners' abandoning their pets, we hope that you will make a valiant effort to solve your Australian Cattle Dog's problems. Patience and understanding are virtues that must dwell in every pet-loving household.

SEPARATION ANXIETY

Recognized by behaviorists as the most common form of stress for dogs, separation anxiety can also lead to destructive behaviors in your dog. It's more than your AuCaDo's howling his displeasure at your leaving the house and his being left alone. This is a normal reaction, no different than the child who cries as his mother leaves him on the first day at school. Separation anxiety is more serious. In fact, if you are constantly with your dog, he will come to expect you with him all of the time, making it even more traumatic for him when you are not there.

Obviously, you enjoy spending time with your dog, and he thrives on your love and attention. However, it should not become a dependent relationship in which he is heartbroken without you. This broken heart can also bring on destructive behavior as well as loss of appetite, depression and lack of interest in play and interaction. Canine behaviorists have been spending much time and energy to help owners better understand the significance of this stressful condition.

One thing you can do to minimize separation anxiety is to make your entrances and exits as low-key as possible. Do not give your dog a long drawn-out goodbye, and do not lavish him with hugs and kisses when you return. This is giving in to the attention that he craves, and it will only make him miss it more when you are away. Another thing you can try is to give your dog a treat when you leave; this will not only keep him occupied and keep

"LONELY WOLF"
The number of dogs that suffer from separation anxiety is on the rise as more and more pet owners find themselves at work all day. New attention is being paid to this problem, which is especially hard to diagnose since it is only evident when the dog is alone. Research is currently being done to help educate dog owners about separation anxiety and how they can help minimize this problem in their dogs.

his mind off the fact that you have just left, but it will also help him associate your leaving with a pleasant experience.

You may have to accustom your dog to being left alone in intervals. Of course, when your dog starts whimpering as you approach the door, your first instinct will be to run to him and comfort him, but do not do it!

Eventually he will adjust to your absence. His anxiety stems from being placed in an unfamiliar situation; by familiarizing him with being alone, he will learn that he will survive. That is not to say you should purposely leave your dog home alone, but the dog needs to know that, while he can depend on you for his care, you do not have to be by his side 24 hours a day. Some behaviorists recommend tiring the dog out before you leave home—take him for a good long walk or engage him in a game of fetch in the yard.

When the dog is alone in the house, he should be placed in his crate—another distinct advantage to crate training your dog. The crate should be placed in his happy family area, where he normally sleeps and already feels comfortable, thereby making him feel more at ease when he is alone. Be sure to give the dog a special chew toy to enjoy while he settles into his crate.

AGGRESSION

This is a problem that concerns all responsible dog owners. Aggression can be a very big problem in dogs, and, when not controlled, always becomes dangerous. An aggressive dog, no matter the size, may lunge at, bite or even attack a person or another dog. Aggressive behavior is not to be tolerated. It is more than just inappropriate behavior; it is

> **TUG-OF-WAR**
> You should never play tug-of-war games with your puppy. Such games create a struggle for "top dog" position and teach the puppy that it is okay to challenge you. It will also encourage your puppy's natural tendency to bite down hard and *win*.

painful for a family to watch their dog become unpredictable in his behavior to the point where they are afraid of him. While not all aggressive behavior is dangerous, things like growling, baring teeth, etc. can be frightening. It is important to ascertain why the dog is acting in this manner. Aggression is a display of dominance, and the dog should not have the dominant role in his pack, which is, in this case, your family.

It is important not to challenge an aggressive dog, as this could provoke an attack. Observe your Australian Cattle Dog's body language. Does he make direct eye contact and stare? Does he try to make himself as large as possible: ears pricked, chest out, tail erect? Height and size signify authority in a dog pack—being taller or "above" another dog literally means that he is "above" in social status. These body signals tell you that your AuCaDo thinks he is in charge, a problem that needs to be addressed. An aggressive dog is unpredictable; you never know when he is going to strike and what he is going to do. You cannot understand why a dog that is playful one minute is growling the next.

Fear is a common cause of aggression in dogs. Perhaps your Australian Cattle Dog had a negative experience as a puppy, which causes him to be fearful when a similar situation presents itself later in life. The dog may act aggressively in order to protect himself from whatever is making him afraid. It is not always easy to determine what is making your dog fearful, but if you can isolate what brings out the fear reaction, you can help the dog get over it.

Supervise your AuCaDo's interactions with people and other dogs, and praise the dog when it goes well. If he starts to act aggressively in a situation, correct him and remove him from the situation. Do not let people approach the dog and start petting him without your express permission. That way, you can have the dog sit to accept petting, and praise him when he behaves properly. You are focusing on praise and on modifying his behavior by rewarding him when he acts appropriately. By being gentle and by supervising his interactions, you are showing him that there is no need to be afraid or defensive.

The best solution is to consult a behavioral specialist, one who has experience with the Australian Cattle Dog if possible. Together, perhaps you can pinpoint the cause of your dog's aggression and do something about it. An aggressive dog cannot be trusted, and a dog that cannot be trusted is not safe to have as a family pet. If, very unusually, you find that your pet has become untrustworthy and you feel it necessary to seek a new home with a more suitable family and environment, explain fully to the new owners all of your reasons for rehoming the dog to be fair to all concerned.

AGGRESSION TOWARD OTHER DOGS
A dog's aggressive behavior toward another dog stems from not enough exposure to other dogs at an early age. If other dogs make your Australian Cattle Dog nervous and agitated, he will lash

---

I'M HOME!
Dogs left alone for varying lengths of time may often react wildly when their owners return. Sometimes they run, jump, bite, chew, tear things apart, wet themselves, gobble their food or behave in other very undisciplined ways. If your dog behaves in this manner upon your return home, allow him to calm down before greeting him or he will consider your attention as a reward for his antics.

Body language says a lot about a dog's attitude. Exposing the belly is a submissive posture, showing that this AuCaDo is comfortable around his friends.

out as a protective mechanism. A dog that has not received sufficient exposure to other canines tends to think that he is the only dog on the planet. The animal becomes so dominant that he does not even show signs that he is fearful or threatened. Without growling or any other physical signal as a warning, he will lunge at and bite the other dog.

SMILE!

Dogs and humans may be the only animals that smile. A dog will imitate the smile on his owner's face when he greets a friend. The dog only smiles at his human friends; he never smiles at another dog or cat. Usually, a dog rolls up his lips and shows his teeth in a clenched mouth while rolling over onto his back, begging for a soft scratch.

A way to correct this is to let your AuCaDo approach another dog when walking on lead. Watch very closely and, at the first sign of aggression, correct your AuCaDo and pull him away. Scold him for any sign of discomfort, and then praise him when he ignores the other dog. Keep this up until either he stops the aggressive behavior, learns to ignore other dogs or even accepts other dogs. Praise him lavishly for his correct behavior.

DOMINANT AGGRESSION

A social hierarchy is firmly established in a wild dog pack. The dog wants to dominate those under him and please those above him. Dogs know that there must be a leader. If you are not the obvious choice for emperor, the dog will assume the throne! These conflicting innate desires are what a dog owner is up against when he sets about training a dog. In training a dog to obey commands, the owner is reinforcing that he is the top dog in the "pack" and that the dog should, and should want to, serve his superior. Thus, the owner is suppressing the dog's urge to dominate by modifying his behavior and making him obedient.

An important part of training is taking every opportunity to reinforce that you are the leader. The simple action of making your Australian Cattle Dog sit to wait for his food instead of allowing him to run up to get it when he wants it says that you control when he eats; he is dependent on you for food. Although it may be difficult, do not give in to your dog's wishes every time he whines at you or looks at you with pleading eyes. It is a constant effort to show the dog

that his place in the pack is at the bottom.

This is not meant to sound cruel or inhumane. You love your Australian Cattle Dog and you should treat him with care and affection. You (hopefully) did not get a dog just so you could control another creature. Dog training is not about being cruel, it is about molding the dog's behavior into what is acceptable and teaching him to live by your rules. In theory, it is quite simple: catch him in appropriate behavior and reward him for it. Add a dog into the equation and it becomes a bit more trying, but as a rule of thumb, positive reinforcement is what works best.

With a dominant dog, punishment and negative reinforcement can have the opposite effect of what you are after. It can make a dog fearful and/or act out aggres-

There is no better exercise for a dog than another dog! Running, chasing and roughhousing games are friendly and energy-expending interactions between canine companions.

sively if he feels he is being challenged. Remember, a dominant dog perceives himself at the top of the social heap, and will fight to defend his perceived status. The best way to prevent that is to never give him reason to think that he is in control in the first place.

If you are having trouble training your Australian Cattle Dog and it seems as if he is constantly challenging your authority, seek the help of an obedience trainer or behavioral specialist. A professional will work with both you and your dog to teach you effective techniques to use at home. Beware of trainers who rely on excessively harsh methods; scolding is necessary now and then, but the focus in your training should always be on positive reinforcement.

SEXUAL BEHAVIOR

Dogs exhibit certain sexual behaviors that may have influenced your choice of male or female when you first purchased your AuCaDo. To a certain extent, spaying/neutering will eliminate these behaviors, but if you are purchasing a dog that you wish to breed from, you should be aware of what you will have to deal with throughout the dog's life.

Female dogs usually have two estruses per year, with each season lasting about three weeks. These are the only times in which

---

THE MIGHTY MALE

Males, whether castrated or not, will mount almost anything: a pillow, your leg or, much to your dismay, even your neighbor's leg. As with other types of inappropriate behavior, the dog must be corrected while in the act, which for once is not difficult. Often he will not let go! While a puppy is experimenting with his very first urges, his owners feel he needs to "sow his oats" and allow the pup to mount. As the pup grows into a full-size dog, with full-size urges, it becomes a nuisance and an embarrassment. Males always appear as if they are trying to "save the race," more determined and stronger than imaginable. While altering the dog at an appropriate age will limit the dog's desire, it usually does not remove it entirely.

---

a female dog will mate, and she usually will not allow this until the second week of the cycle, although this varies from bitch to bitch. If not bred during the heat cycle, it is not uncommon for a bitch to experience a false pregnancy, in which her mammary glands swell and she exhibits maternal tendencies toward toys or other objects.

With male dogs, owners must be aware that whole dogs (dogs who are not neutered) have the natural inclination to mark their territory. Males mark their territory by spraying small amounts of urine as they lift their legs in a macho ritual. Marking can occur both outdoors in the yard and around the neighborhood as well as indoors on furniture legs, curtains and the sofa. Such behavior can be very frustrating for the owner; early training is strongly urged before the "urge" strikes your dog. Neutering the male at an appropriate early age can solve this problem before it becomes a habit.

Other problems associated with males are wandering and mounting. Both of these habits, of course, belong to the unneutered dog, whose sexual drive leads him away from home in search of the bitch in heat. Males will mount females in heat, as well as any other dog, male or female, that happens to catch their fancy. Other possible mounting partners include his owner, the furniture, guests to the home and strangers on the street. Discourage such behavior early on.

Owners must further recognize that mounting is not merely a sexual expression but also one of dominance, seen in males and females alike. Be consistent and be persistent, and you will find that you can "move mounters."

CHEWING

The national canine pastime is chewing! Every dog loves to sink his "canines" into a tasty bone (or whatever is available), so it is important to provide your dog with appropriate chew toys so that he doesn't destroy your possessions or make a habit of gnawing on your hands and fingers. Dogs need to chew to massage their gums, to make their new teeth feel better and to exercise their jaws. This is a natural behavior that is deeply embedded in all things canine. Our role as owners is not to stop the dog's chewing, but rather to redirect it to positive, chew-

---

"X" MARKS THE SPOT

As a pack animal, your dog marks his territory as a way of letting any possible intruders know that this is his space and that he will defend his territory if necessary. Your dog marks by urinating because urine contains pheromones that allow other canines to identify him. While this behavior seems like a nuisance, it speaks volumes about your dog's mental health. Stable, well-trained dogs living in quiet, less populated areas may mark less frequently than less confident dogs inhabiting busy urban areas that attract many possible invaders. If your dog only marks in certain areas in your home, your bed or just the front door, these are the areas he feels obligated to defend. If your dog marks frequently, see your veterinarian or an animal behaviorist.

worthy objects. Be an informed owner and purchase proper chew toys, like strong nylon bones, that will not splinter. Be sure that the objects are safe and durable, since your dog's safety is at risk. Again, the owner is responsible for ensuring a dog-proof environment.

The best answer is prevention; that is, put your shoes, handbags and other tasty objects in their proper places (out of the reach of the growing canine mouth). Direct your puppy to his toys whenever you see him "tasting" the furniture legs or the leg of your trousers. Make a loud noise to attract the pup's attention and immediately escort him to his chew toy and engage him with the toy for at least four minutes, praising and encouraging him all the while. An array of safe, interesting chew toys will keep your dog's mind and teeth occupied, and distracted from chewing on things he shouldn't.

Some trainers recommend deterrents, such as hot pepper, a bitter spice or a product designed for this purpose, to discourage the dog from chewing unwanted objects. Test these products to see which works best before investing in large quantities.

JUMPING UP

Jumping up is a dog's friendly way of saying hello! Some dog owners do not mind when their

NO JUMPING

Stop a dog from jumping up before he jumps. If he is getting ready to jump onto you, simply walk away. If he jumps up on you before you can turn away, lift your knee so that it bumps him in the chest. Do not be forceful. Your dog soon will realize that jumping up is not a productive way of getting attention.

dog jumps up. The problem arises when guests come to the house and the dog greets them in the same manner—whether they like it or not! However friendly the greeting may be, the chances are that your visitors will not appreciate your dog's enthusiasm. The dog will not be able to distinguish upon whom he can jump and whom he cannot. Therefore, it is probably best to discourage this behavior entirely.

Pick a command such as "Off" (avoid using "Down" since you will use that for the dog to lie down) and tell him "Off" when he jumps up. Place him on the ground on all fours and have him sit, praising him the whole time.

Always lavish him with praise and petting when he is in the sit position. In this way, you can give him a warm affectionate greeting, let him know that you are as excited to see him as he is to see you and instill good manners at the same time!

DIGGING

Digging, which is seen as a destructive behavior to humans, is actually quite a natural behavior in dogs. Although terriers (the "earth dogs") are most associated with digging, any dog's desire to dig can be irrepressible and most frustrating to his owners. When digging occurs in your yard, it is actually a normal behavior redirected into something the dog can do in his everyday life. In the wild, a dog would be actively seeking food, making his own shelter, etc. He would be using his paws in a purposeful manner for his survival. Since you provide him with food and shelter, he has no need to use his paws for these purposes, and so the energy that he would be using may manifest itself in the form of little holes all over your yard and flower beds.

Perhaps your dog is digging as a reaction to boredom—it is somewhat similar to someone eating a whole bag of chips in front of the TV—because they are

About to get his paws dirty, this AuCaDo investigates to find a pleasing place to dig.

there and there is nothing better to do! Basically, the answer is to provide the dog with adequate play and exercise so that his mind and paws are occupied, and so that he feels as if he is doing something useful.

Of course, digging is easiest to control if it is stopped as soon as possible, but it is often hard to catch a dog in the act. If your dog is a compulsive digger and is not easily distracted by other activities, you can designate an area on your property where he is allowed to dig. If you catch him digging in an off-limits area of the yard, immediately take him to the approved area and praise him for digging there. Keep a close eye on him so that you can catch him in the act—that is the only way to make him understand what is permitted and what is not. If you take him to a hole he dug an hour ago and tell him "No," he will understand that you are not fond of holes, dirt or flowers. If you catch him while he is stifle-deep in your tulips, that is when he will get your message.

BARKING

Dogs cannot talk—oh, what they would say if they could! Instead, barking is a dog's way of "talking." It can be somewhat frustrating because it is not always easy to tell what a dog means by his bark—is he excited, happy, frightened or angry?

Whatever it is that the dog is trying to say, he should not be punished for barking. It is only when the barking becomes excessive, and when the excessive barking becomes a bad habit, that the behavior needs to be modified.

Fortunately, Australian Cattle Dogs are not as vocal as most other dogs; they tend to use their barks more purposefully. If an intruder came into your home in the middle of the night and your AuCaDo barked a warning, wouldn't you be pleased? You would probably deem your dog a hero, a wonderful guardian and protector of the home. On the other hand, if a friend drops by unexpectedly, rings the doorbell and is greeted with a sudden sharp bark, you would probably be annoyed at the dog. But in reality, isn't this just the same behavior? The dog does not know any better. Unless he sees who is at the door and it is someone he knows, he will bark as a means of vocalizing that his (and your)

DON'T PUCKER UP
We all love our dogs and our dogs love us. They show their love and affection by licking us. This is not a very sanitary practice, as dogs lick and sniff in some unsavory places. Kissing your dog on the mouth is strictly forbidden, as parasites can be transmitted in this manner.

territory is being threatened. While your friend is not posing a threat, it is all the same to the dog. Barking is his means of letting you know that there is an intrusion, whether friend or foe, on your property. This type of barking is instinctive and should not be discouraged.

Excessive habitual barking, however, is a problem that should be corrected early on. As your Australian Cattle Dog grows up, you will be able to tell when his barking is purposeful and when it is for no reason. You will become able to distinguish your dog's different barks and their meanings. For example, the bark when someone comes to the door will be different than the bark when he is excited to see you. It is similar to a person's tone of voice, except that the dog has to rely totally on tone of voice because he does not have the benefit of using words. An incessant barker will be evident at an early age.

There are some things that encourage a dog to bark. For example, if your dog barks non-stop for a few minutes and you give him a treat to quiet him, he believes that you are rewarding him for barking. He will associate barking with getting a treat and will keep doing it until he is rewarded. On the other hand, if you give him a command such as "Quiet" and praise him after he has stopped barking for a few

> **BARKING STANCE**
> Did you know that a dog is less likely to bark when sitting than standing? Watch your dog the next time that you suspect he is about to start barking. You'll notice that as he does, he gets up on all four feet. Hence, when teaching a dog to stop barking, it helps to get him to sit before you command him to be quiet.

seconds, he will get the idea that being "quiet" is what you want him to do.

FOOD STEALING

Is your dog devising ways of stealing food from your coffee table or kitchen counter? If so, you must answer the following questions: Is your Australian Cattle Dog a bit hungry, or is he "constantly famished" like many dogs seem to be? Face it, some dogs are more food-motivated than others. They are totally obsessed by the smell of food and can only think of their next meal. Food stealing is terrific fun and always yields a great reward— *food*, glorious food.

Your goal as an owner, therefore, is to be sensible about where food is placed in the home and to reprimand your dog whenever he is caught in the act of stealing. But remember, only reprimand your dog if you actually see him stealing, not later

The Australian Cattle dog greets every day and every situation with an alert eye and a keen mind, ready for action!

when the crime is discovered; that will be of no use at all and will only serve to confuse him.

BEGGING

Just like food stealing, begging is a favorite pastime of hungry puppies! It achieves that same terrific result—food! Dogs quickly learn that their owners keep the "good food" for ourselves, and that we humans do not dine on dry food alone. Begging is a conditioned response related to a specific stimulus, time and place. The sounds of the kitchen, cans and bottles opening, crinkling bags, the smell of food in preparation, etc., will excite the dog, and soon the paws will be in the air!

Here is the solution to stopping this behavior: Never give

in to a beggar! You are rewarding the dog for sitting pretty, jumping up, whining and rubbing his nose into you by giving him food. By ignoring the dog, you will (eventually) force the behavior into extinction. Note that the behavior is likely to get worse before it disappears, so be sure there are not any "softies" in the family who will give in to little "Oliver" every time he whimpers, "More, please."

COPROPHAGIA
Feces eating is, to humans, one of the most disgusting behaviors that their dogs could engage in; yet, to dogs, it is perfectly normal. It is hard for us to understand why a dog would want to eat his own feces. He could be seeking certain nutrients that are missing from his diet, he could be just hungry or he could be attracted by the pleasing (to a dog) scent. While coprophagia most often refers to the dog's eating his own feces, a dog may just as likely eat that of another animal as well, if he comes across it. Dogs often find the stool of cats and horses more palatable than that of other dogs.

Vets have found that diets with low levels of digestibility, containing relatively low levels of fiber and high levels of starch, increase coprophagia. Therefore, high-fiber diets may decrease the likelihood of dogs' eating feces. Both the consistency of the stool

---

AIN'T MISBEHAVIN'
Punishment is rarely necessary for a misbehaving dog. Dogs that habitually behave badly probably had a poor education and do not know what is expected of them. They need training. Negative reinforcement on your part usually does more harm than good.

(how firm it feels in the dog's mouth) and the presence of undigested nutrients increase the likelihood. Once the dog develops diarrhea from feces eating, he will likely stop this distasteful habit.

To discourage this behavior, first make sure that the food you are feeding your dog is nutritionally complete and that he is getting enough food. If changes in his diet do not seem to work, and no medical cause can be found, you will have to modify the behavior through environmental control before it becomes a habit. The best way to prevent your dog from eating feces is to make it unavailable—clean up after he eliminates and remove any stool from the yard or litter box. If it is not there, he cannot eat it.

Reprimanding for stool eating rarely impresses the dog. Vets recommend distracting the dog while he is in the act of stool eating. Coprophagia is seen most frequently in pups 6 to 12 months of age, and usually disappears around the dog's first birthday.

My Australian Cattle Dog

PUT YOUR PUPPY'S FIRST PICTURE HERE

Dog's Name _____

Date _____ Photographer _____